3 Days Guide in Coimbra

via Sandra Filipe Photography

Welcome to Coimbra and Aveiro, two of the most charming and picturesque cities in Portugal! Coimbra is a city that boasts a rich history and vibrant student life, while Aveiro is famous for its colorful architecture and the beauty of its canals. Together, they offer a unique and unforgettable travel experience that will leave you wanting more.

In this travel guide, we will take you on a journey through these two cities, providing you with insider tips and recommendations on the best places to visit, eat, and stay. From historic monasteries and libraries to delicious pastries and wines, there is something for everyone in Coimbra and Aveiro.

So pack your bags, grab your camera, and get ready for an adventure you won't soon forget!

Contents

3 Days Guide in Coimbra & Aveiro, Portugal 1

I. Introduction 5

    Overview of Coimbra and Aveiro 5

    Why visit Coimbra and Aveiro? 5

II. Getting to Coimbra and Aveiro 7

    By Plane: 7

    By Train: 7

    By Bus: 8

    By Car: 8

III. Coimbra 10

    History and Culture 10

    Top Attractions 11

    Museums 13

    Food and Drink 16

    Nightlife 18

    Where to Stay in Coimbra 21

IV. Aveiro 23

    History and Culture 23

    Top Attractions 26

    Food and Drink 28

    Nightlife 30

    Where to Stay in Aveiro 31

V. Day Trips from Coimbra and Aveiro 33

    Figueira da Foz 33

    Bussaco Palace and National Forest 34

    Praia da Barra 36

Ílhavo Maritime Museum 37

VI. Practical Information 39

Weather and Best Time to Visit 39

How to Get Around 40

Safety Tips 43

Useful Apps for your Visit 44

Useful Phrases 45

A 3-Day Itinerary for First Timers 47

Day 1: Arrival, Top Monuments 47

1st Day in Coimbra – Map 51

ZoomTip 1.1: Transportation 52

ZoomTip 1.2: Information on the Monuments 53

Sé Velha Church 53

National Museum Machado de Castro 54

Sé Nova Church 55

Porta Férrea & School's Courtyard 55

Joanina Library 56

 Cabra – University Tower......................................57

Aqueduct of St. Sebastian 58

ZoomTip 1.3: Tapas Nas Costas 59

Day 2: Morning in Coimbra / Arrival in Aveiro 60

Aliança Underground Museum 62

Coimbra and Aveiro 2nd Day Map 64

ZoomTip 2.3: Information on the Monuments 65

Monastery of Santa Clara 65

Monastery of Santa Cruz 66

Museum of Aveiro 67

Day 3: Cathedral, Moliceiro Cruise and Costa Nova Area 68

Aveiro 3rd Day Map – Zoomed Out 70

Zoom Tip 3.1: Information on the Attractions 71

Cathedral of Aveiro 71

Moliceiro Cruise 71

Costa Nova 72

Zoom Tip 3.2: Mercado do Peixe Restaurant..............................73   74

Food Dishes and Drinks to Try While You are at Coimbra and Aveiro .74

Thank you! 84

I. Introduction

Overview of Coimbra and Aveiro

Located in the central region of Portugal, Coimbra and Aveiro are two beautiful and historic cities that are worth a visit for any traveler. Coimbra is known for its rich academic history and stunning architecture, while Aveiro is renowned for its picturesque canals and beautiful beaches.

Coimbra is the fourth largest city in Portugal and has been the country's capital in the past. It is home to one of the oldest and most prestigious universities in Europe, the University of Coimbra, which was founded in 1290. The city is full of narrow streets, historic buildings, and beautiful gardens, making it a charming place to visit.

On the other hand, Aveiro is a small but picturesque city located on the coast of Portugal. It is often called the "Venice of Portugal" because of its winding canals that run through the city center. The city is also known for its stunning beaches, including the popular Costa Nova beach, which is lined with colorful striped houses.

Overall, Coimbra and Aveiro offer visitors a perfect mix of history, culture, and natural beauty. Both cities are relatively small and easy to navigate, making them ideal for a day trip or weekend getaway.

Why visit Coimbra and Aveiro?

Coimbra and Aveiro have a lot to offer travelers, from stunning architecture and rich history to beautiful beaches and natural landscapes.

Here are a few reasons why you should consider visiting Coimbra and Aveiro:

1. **History and Culture:** Coimbra is home to one of the oldest universities in Europe, and the city's historic center is full of stunning medieval and Renaissance buildings. Aveiro, on the other hand, has a rich maritime history and is famous for its traditional moliceiros boats, which were used for harvesting seaweed.

2. **Architecture:** Both cities are full of stunning examples of Portuguese architecture, from the Baroque-style Biblioteca Joanina in Coimbra to the colorful striped houses of Costa Nova in Aveiro.
3. **Natural Beauty:** Coimbra and Aveiro are surrounded by beautiful natural landscapes, including the Serra da Estrela mountain range and the Ria de Aveiro lagoon. There are also plenty of beautiful beaches to explore, including Praia da Barra and the beaches of Figueira da Foz.
4. **Food and Drink:** Portugal is famous for its delicious food and wine, and Coimbra and Aveiro are no exception. Visitors can try local specialties such as Cozido à Portuguesa (a hearty meat and vegetable stew) in Coimbra, and fresh seafood in Aveiro.
5. **Accessibility:** Coimbra and Aveiro are both easily accessible by train or bus from major Portuguese cities such as Lisbon and Porto, making them ideal for a day trip or weekend getaway.

Overall, Coimbra and Aveiro are two charming and historic cities that offer visitors a chance to experience the best of Portugal's culture, history, and natural beauty.

II. Getting to Coimbra and Aveiro

Coimbra and Aveiro are both located in central Portugal and are easily accessible by plane, train, bus, or car. Here's everything you need to know about getting to these two cities.

By Plane:

The nearest airport to Coimbra and Aveiro is the Francisco Sá Carneiro Airport in Porto, which is about 120 km away. The airport is well-connected to major European cities and offers direct flights to and from several destinations around the world.

From the airport, you can take a direct train or bus to Coimbra or Aveiro. Alternatively, you can rent a car or take a taxi, although this can be quite expensive.

Website: https://www.aeroportoporto.pt/en/

Prices: A one-way ticket from Porto to Coimbra or Aveiro costs around €12-€20 for a train and €10-€15 for a bus. A taxi ride can cost up to €150.

Useful Info: Be aware of the luggage restrictions on trains and buses, and make sure to book your tickets in advance to secure a seat.

By Train:

Coimbra and Aveiro are both well-connected by train to major cities in Portugal, including Lisbon and Porto. The train stations are located in the city center, making it easy to reach your destination.

The train ride from Lisbon to Coimbra takes about two hours, while the train ride from Porto to Aveiro takes about 50 minutes. Trains are comfortable, reliable, and affordable, making them a popular choice for travelers.

Website: https://www.cp.pt/passageiros/en/

Prices: A one-way ticket from Lisbon to Coimbra costs around €20-€30, while a ticket from Porto to Aveiro costs around €5-€10.

Useful Info: It's best to book your tickets in advance, especially during peak travel season. You can also purchase tickets online, at train stations, or through travel agencies.

By Bus:

Coimbra and Aveiro are also well-connected by bus to major cities in Portugal, including Lisbon and Porto. Buses are usually cheaper than trains, although they can take longer to reach their destination.

The bus ride from Lisbon to Coimbra takes about three hours, while the bus ride from Porto to Aveiro takes about one hour. Buses are comfortable and usually have air conditioning, making them a good option for budget-conscious travelers.

Website: https://www.rede-expressos.pt/en/

Prices: A one-way ticket from Lisbon to Coimbra costs around €10-€20, while a ticket from Porto to Aveiro costs around €5-€10.

Useful Info: Book your tickets in advance to secure a seat, especially during peak travel season. Buses may also have limited luggage space, so be aware of the luggage restrictions.

By Car:

Driving to Coimbra and Aveiro is a good option if you want to explore the surrounding areas or if you have a lot of luggage. Rental cars are available at major airports and cities in Portugal, and the roads are generally in good condition.

The drive from Lisbon to Coimbra takes about two hours, while the drive from Porto to Aveiro takes about 45 minutes. However, be aware that parking in city centers can be difficult and expensive.

Website: https://www.rentalcars.com/

Prices: Rental car prices vary depending on the type of car and the duration of the rental.

Useful Info: Be aware of the toll roads in Portugal, which require an electronic toll device (called a Via Verde). You can rent a device from the car rental company or purchase a temporary one at a post office or gas station. Also, make sure to familiarize yourself with the driving laws and regulations in Portugal, such as speed limits and traffic signs.

Overall, driving to Coimbra and Aveiro is a good option if you want to explore the surrounding areas or if you have a lot of luggage. However, if you plan to stay in the city center, it may be more convenient to use public transportation.

Useful Info:

- Coimbra and Aveiro are well-connected by public transportation, making it easy to travel between the two cities.

- Tickets for trains and buses can be purchased online, at train stations or bus terminals, or through travel agencies.

- It's best to book your tickets in advance, especially during peak travel season.

- Luggage restrictions may apply on trains and buses, so be aware of the rules and regulations.

- If you plan to rent a car, be aware of the toll roads and driving laws in Portugal.

- Parking in city centers can be difficult and expensive, so consider staying in a hotel outside the city center and using public transportation to get around.

In conclusion, Coimbra and Aveiro are easily accessible by plane, train, bus, or car. Whether you're looking for convenience, affordability, or adventure, there's a transportation option that will suit your needs.

III. Coimbra

Coimbra is a charming and historic city located in central Portugal, known for its rich academic history and stunning architecture. It is home to one of the oldest universities in Europe, the University of Coimbra, which has been a center of learning and culture for over 700 years. The city's historic center is full of narrow streets, colorful buildings, and beautiful gardens, making it a delight to explore. In this section, we'll delve into the history and culture of Coimbra, exploring its most important landmarks, museums, and traditions.

History and Culture

Coimbra has a long and fascinating history that dates back to the Roman era. The city was an important center of commerce and culture during the Middle Ages, and in 1139 it became the capital of Portugal. During this time, Coimbra was known for its thriving intellectual and artistic community, which produced some of the most important works of literature, music, and art in Portuguese history.

One of the most important landmarks in Coimbra is the University of Coimbra, which was founded in 1290 by King Dinis. The university was originally located in Lisbon, but it was moved to Coimbra in 1537 and has been located there ever since. Today, the University of Coimbra is one of the oldest and most prestigious universities in Europe, and it attracts students from all over the world.

Another important landmark in Coimbra is the Biblioteca Joanina, a stunning Baroque-style library that was built in the 18th century. The library is home to over 200,000 volumes, including some of the rarest and most valuable books in the world. Visitors can admire the library's ornate decoration, which includes gilded shelves, intricate carvings, and stunning frescoes.

The Sé Velha, or Old Cathedral, is another must-see landmark in Coimbra. The cathedral was built in the Romanesque style in the 12th century, and it is one of the most important examples of this style of architecture in Portugal. The cathedral is known for its beautiful rose window, stunning cloisters, and rich history.

One of the most important museums in Coimbra is the Machado de Castro National Museum, which is housed in a former bishop's palace.

The museum contains an impressive collection of Portuguese art and artifacts, including Roman and medieval sculptures, Baroque paintings, and traditional crafts.

Coimbra is also known for its traditional music and dance, which are an important part of Portuguese culture. Fado de Coimbra is a unique style of fado, a traditional Portuguese music genre that is characterized by its melancholic melodies and lyrics. Fado de Coimbra is performed exclusively by male singers, and it is often accompanied by guitar and mandolin.

Finally, Coimbra is known for its delicious cuisine, which is based on fresh ingredients and traditional cooking methods. Local specialties include Cozido à Portuguesa, a hearty meat and vegetable stew, and Queijo da Serra, a soft and creamy cheese that is made in the nearby mountains.

Overall, Coimbra is a city rich in history, culture, and tradition. From its stunning landmarks and museums to its traditional music and delicious cuisine, there's something for everyone in this charming Portuguese city.

Top Attractions

Coimbra is a charming city located in central Portugal that is known for its rich academic history, stunning architecture, and vibrant culture. In this section, we'll explore the top attractions in Coimbra, including the University of Coimbra, Biblioteca Joanina, Sé Velha, and Monastery of Santa Clara-a-Velha.

University of Coimbra

The University of Coimbra is one of the oldest and most prestigious universities in Europe, and it has been a center of learning and culture for over 700 years. The university was founded in 1290 by King Dinis, and it originally served as a center of theological and legal education.

Today, the University of Coimbra is a thriving academic institution that attracts students from all over the world. The university is located on a hill overlooking the city, and it is surrounded by stunning architecture, beautiful gardens, and panoramic views of the surrounding countryside.

One of the most impressive buildings on the university campus is the Paço das Escolas, which is home to several important faculties, including law, medicine, and humanities. Visitors can also explore the Capela de São Miguel, a stunning Baroque-style chapel that is decorated with beautiful frescoes and sculptures.

Another must-see attraction at the University of Coimbra is the Biblioteca Geral, which is one of the oldest and most beautiful libraries in the world. The library contains over a million books, manuscripts, and other rare documents, and it is famous for its stunning Baroque-style decoration and intricate carvings.

Biblioteca Joanina

The Biblioteca Joanina is one of the most beautiful libraries in the world, and it is a must-see attraction for any visitor to Coimbra. The library was built in the 18th century and is named after King João V, who commissioned its construction.

The library is located on the university campus and is famous for its stunning Baroque-style decoration, including gilded shelves, intricate carvings, and beautiful frescoes. Visitors can admire the library's ornate decoration, as well as its impressive collection of rare books and manuscripts.

One of the most impressive features of the Biblioteca Joanina is its colony of bats, which were introduced to the library in the 18th century to protect the books from insects. Today, the bats are an important part of the library's ecosystem and are protected as a national heritage.

Sé Velha

The Sé Velha, or Old Cathedral, is one of the most important landmarks in Coimbra and is a must-see attraction for any visitor to the city. The cathedral was built in the Romanesque style in the 12th century and is one of the most important examples of this style of architecture in Portugal.

The cathedral is located in the historic center of Coimbra and is known for its beautiful rose window, stunning cloisters, and rich history.

Visitors can explore the cathedral's interior, which is filled with beautiful frescoes, sculptures, and other works of art.

One of the most impressive features of the Sé Velha is its beautiful cloisters, which date back to the 13th century. The cloisters are decorated with stunning sculptures and beautiful gardens, making them a peaceful and picturesque place to relax.

Monastery of Santa Clara-a-Velha

The Monastery of Santa Clara-a-Velha is a beautiful and historic monastery that is located on the banks of the Mondego River in Coimbra. The monastery was founded in the 14th century and was once an important center of worship and pilgrimage.

Today, the Monastery of Santa Clara-a-Velha is a popular tourist attraction and is known for its beautiful architecture and stunning views of the river. Visitors can explore the monastery's interior, which contains beautiful Gothic-style arches, vaulted ceilings, and intricate carvings.

One of the most interesting features of the Monastery of Santa Clara-a-Velha is its underground museum, which showcases the history and archeology of the monastery. Visitors can explore the museum's exhibits, which include artifacts and objects from the medieval period, as well as interactive displays and multimedia installations.

Another popular attraction at the Monastery of Santa Clara-a-Velha is the nearby Santa Clara Bridge, which offers stunning views of the monastery and the river. Visitors can walk across the bridge and admire the beautiful scenery, or relax in one of the nearby cafes or restaurants.

Overall, Coimbra is a city that is full of history, culture, and tradition, and these four attractions are just a few of the many things to see and do in this beautiful Portuguese city. Whether you're interested in exploring the city's academic history, admiring its stunning architecture, or simply relaxing by the river, there's something for everyone in Coimbra.

Museums

Coimbra is a city rich in history and culture, and there are several museums in the city that showcase the region's art, history, and traditions. In this section, we'll explore the top museums in Coimbra, including their top exhibits, website, ticket prices, and address.

1. Machado de Castro National Museum:

The Machado de Castro National Museum is one of the most important museums in Coimbra and is housed in a former bishop's palace in the historic center of the city. The museum contains an impressive collection of Portuguese art and artifacts, including Roman and medieval sculptures, Baroque paintings, and traditional crafts.

Top Exhibits:
- The Gothic tombs of King Afonso IV and Queen Beatriz
- The 16th-century tapestries depicting the Conquest of Tunis
- The 17th-century Baroque altarpieces from the church of Santa Cruz

Website: https://www.museumachadocastro.gov.pt/en
Ticket Price: €6 for adults, €3 for students and seniors
Address: Largo Dr. José Rodrigues, 3000-236 Coimbra, Portugal

2. Science Museum of the University of Coimbra:

The Science Museum of the University of Coimbra is located on the university campus and is dedicated to showcasing the history and development of science and technology. The museum has a range of exhibits, including interactive displays, multimedia installations, and historical artifacts.

Top Exhibits:
- The Foucault pendulum, which demonstrates the rotation of the earth
- The collection of scientific instruments from the 18th and 19th centuries
- The interactive displays on the history of astronomy and physics

Website: https://www.museudaciencia.org/en
Ticket Price: €4 for adults, €2 for students and seniors
Address: Largo Marquês de Pombal, 3000-272 Coimbra, Portugal

3. National Museum Machado de Castro:

The National Museum Machado de Castro is located in the heart of Coimbra, in a former bishop's palace that was converted into a museum in the 20th century. The museum has a vast collection of art and artifacts from different periods of Portuguese history, including Roman and medieval sculptures, Baroque paintings, and traditional crafts.

Top Exhibits:
- The 17th-century Baroque altarpieces from the church of Santa Cruz
- The Gothic tombs of King Afonso IV and Queen Beatriz
- The 16th-century tapestries depicting the Conquest of Tunis

Website: https://www.museumachadocastro.gov.pt/en
Ticket Price: €6 for adults, €3 for students and seniors
Address: Largo Dr. José Rodrigues, 3000-236 Coimbra, Portugal

4. Fado Museum:

The Fado Museum is located in the historic center of Coimbra and is dedicated to showcasing the history and development of the Fado music genre. The museum has a range of exhibits, including multimedia installations, recordings of famous Fado performers, and a collection of traditional Fado instruments.

Top Exhibits:
- The interactive displays on the history and development of Fado music
- The collection of traditional Fado instruments, including the Portuguese guitar and the mandolin
- The recordings of famous Fado performers, including Amália Rodrigues and Carlos do Carmo
-

Website: http://www.museudofado.pt/

Ticket Price: €5 for adults, €2.50 for students and seniors
Address: Largo do Choupal, 3000-225 Coimbra, Portugal

Overall, Coimbra is a city rich in history and culture, with several museums that offer a glimpse into the region's art, history, and traditions. Whether you're interested in exploring the Gothic tombs of Portuguese royalty, learning about the development of science and technology, or discovering the history of Fado music, there's a museum in Coimbra that will suit your interests.

Food and Drink

Portuguese cuisine is known for its bold flavors and fresh ingredients, and Coimbra is no exception. The city has a vibrant culinary scene, with a wide range of restaurants, cafes, and bars offering delicious food and drinks. In this section, we'll explore the best places to eat and drink in Coimbra, as well as some of the city's most popular dishes and drinks.

Top Spots/Suggestions:
1. Taberna Urbana:
Taberna Urbana is a popular restaurant in Coimbra that is known for its modern take on traditional Portuguese cuisine. The restaurant offers a range of dishes, including seafood, meat, and vegetarian options, and everything is made using locally sourced ingredients.
Some of the most popular dishes at Taberna Urbana include the octopus rice, the pork cheeks with sweet potato puree, and the grilled vegetables with goat cheese. The restaurant also has an extensive wine list, with many local wines and international options available.
Website: http://www.tabernaurbana.pt/
Prices: Expect to pay around €20-€30 per person for a meal.

2. A Cozinha da Maria:
A Cozinha da Maria is a cozy and welcoming restaurant in Coimbra that specializes in traditional Portuguese cuisine. The restaurant offers a range of dishes, including grilled meats, fresh seafood, and homemade soups and stews.

Some of the most popular dishes at A Cozinha da Maria include the grilled octopus, the arroz de marisco (seafood rice), and the cozido à portuguesa (meat and vegetable stew). The restaurant also has a selection of homemade desserts, including the popular pastel de nata (Portuguese custard tart).

Website: https://www.facebook.com/acozinhadamariacoimbra/

Prices: Expect to pay around €15-€25 per person for a meal.

3. Café Santa Cruz:

Café Santa Cruz is a historic café in Coimbra that is known for its beautiful architecture, delicious food, and live music. The café has been open since 1923 and has become a popular spot for locals and tourists alike.

Some of the most popular dishes at Café Santa Cruz include the bifanas (pork sandwiches), the cod fritters, and the croquettes. The café also has a range of desserts and pastries, including the popular bola de berlim (Portuguese custard-filled doughnuts).

Website: https://cafesantacruz.com/

Prices: Expect to pay around €10-€20 per person for a meal.

4. Pátio das Cantigas:

Pátio das Cantigas is a popular bar and restaurant in Coimbra that is known for its lively atmosphere and delicious cocktails. The bar offers a range of cocktails and other drinks, as well as a small menu of snacks and light bites.

Some of the most popular cocktails at Pátio das Cantigas include the gin and tonic, the mojito, and the caipirinha. The bar also has a range of local beers and wines available.

Website: https://www.facebook.com/patiodascantigas.coimbra/

Prices: Expect to pay around €5-€10 per cocktail.

Top Dishes/Drinks:
1. Cozido à Portuguesa:

Cozido à Portuguesa is a traditional meat and vegetable stew that is often served during the colder months of the year. The stew usually contains a range of meats, including pork, beef, and chicken, as well as vegetables such as cabbage, carrots, and potatoes.

2. Bacalhau:

Bacalhau, or salt cod, is a popular ingredient in Portuguese cuisine, and there are countless ways to prepare it. Some of the most popular dishes include bacalhau à brás (shredded salt cod with potatoes and eggs), bacalhau com natas (salt cod with cream and potatoes), and bacalhau à Gomes de Sá (salt cod with onions, potatoes, and olives).

3. Queijo da Serra:

Queijo da Serra is a soft and creamy cheese that is made in the nearby Serra da Estrela mountains. The cheese is made using raw sheep's milk and has a slightly tangy flavor that pairs well with bread and wine.

4. Vinho Verde:

Vinho Verde is a light and refreshing wine that is produced in the Minho region of Portugal, which is located north of Coimbra. The wine is known for its crisp acidity and fruity flavors, and it pairs well with a range of dishes.

Useful Info:

- Tipping in restaurants and cafes is not mandatory in Portugal, but it is customary to round up the bill or leave a small tip if you received good service.
- Many restaurants in Coimbra offer a "menu do dia," which is a set menu that includes a starter, main course, and dessert for a fixed price. This can be a great way to try a range of dishes at an affordable price.
- Portuguese dining customs dictate that meals are often enjoyed over a longer period of time, with multiple courses and plenty of conversation. Don't rush your meal, and take the time to savor each dish and enjoy the company of your dining companions.

Overall, Coimbra is a city that is full of delicious food and drink, with a range of restaurants, cafes, and bars offering traditional Portuguese cuisine and international options. Whether you're looking for a hearty stew, fresh seafood, or a refreshing cocktail, there's something for everyone in Coimbra.

Nightlife

Coimbra is a city with a vibrant and exciting nightlife, with plenty of bars, clubs, and music venues that cater to a range of tastes and styles. In this section, we'll explore the top spots for nightlife in Coimbra, including their website, price range, and address.

Top Spots:

1. Praça da República:

Praça da República is the heart of the nightlife scene in Coimbra and is home to several bars and clubs that are popular with locals and tourists alike. The square is lined with outdoor cafes and restaurants, and the area is bustling with people late into the night.

Some of the most popular bars and clubs in Praça da República include:

- Café Santa Cruz: A historic cafe that serves a range of drinks and snacks, and also features live music on select nights.
- Via Latina: A popular bar that serves a range of cocktails and other drinks, as well as light bites and snacks.
- NB Club: A popular nightclub that plays a range of music, including electronic, pop, and hip-hop.

Price Range: Expect to pay around €5-€10 per drink.

Address: Praça da República, 3000-343 Coimbra, Portugal

2. Gin Club:

Gin Club is a popular cocktail bar in Coimbra that specializes in gin-based drinks. The bar has a range of gin brands and flavors available, and the bartenders are skilled at creating unique and delicious cocktails. Some of the most popular drinks at Gin Club include the classic gin and tonic, as well as the bar's own specialty cocktails.

Website: https://www.facebook.com/ginclubcoimbra/

Price Range: Expect to pay around €7-€12 per cocktail.

Address: Rua do Quebra Costas, 3000-340 Coimbra, Portugal

3. Salão Brazil:

Salão Brazil is a cultural center in Coimbra that features a bar, cafe, and music venue. The bar serves a range of drinks, including wine, beer, and cocktails, and the cafe serves light bites and snacks.

The music venue hosts a range of concerts and performances, including jazz, rock, and electronic music.

Website: https://www.facebook.com/salaobrazil/
Price Range: Expect to pay around €5-€10 per drink.
Address: Rua do Quebra Costas, 3000-340 Coimbra, Portugal

4. Fado ao Centro:

Fado ao Centro is a music venue in Coimbra that specializes in Fado music, a traditional Portuguese music genre that is characterized by its soulful melodies and mournful lyrics.

The venue features regular performances by local Fado musicians, as well as workshops and other events related to Fado music.
Website: http://www.fadoaocentro.com/

Price Range: Expect to pay around €15-€20 per ticket for a performance.
Address: Rua Quebra Costas 7/15, 3000-340 Coimbra, Portugal

Overall, Coimbra is a city with a lively and diverse nightlife scene, with plenty of bars, clubs, and music venues that cater to a range of tastes and styles. Whether you're looking to dance the night away or enjoy a relaxed drink with friends, there's a spot in Coimbra that will suit your preferences.

Where to Stay in Coimbra

Coimbra is a popular tourist destination in Portugal, and as such, there are plenty of options for accommodation in the city. Whether you're looking for a luxurious hotel or a budget-friendly hostel, Coimbra has something to offer for every type of traveler. In this section, we'll explore some of the best places to stay in Coimbra, including hotels, hostels, and guesthouses.

Hotels:

Coimbra is home to several top hotels that offer a range of amenities and services, as well as a comfortable and luxurious stay. One of the most popular hotels in the city is the Hotel Quinta das Lágrimas, a luxurious 5-star hotel that is set in a historic palace and features a spa, outdoor pool, and several restaurants. Other popular hotels include the Vila Galé Coimbra, which offers stunning views of the city and the Mondego River, and the Tivoli Coimbra, which is located in the heart of the city and offers easy access to many of its top attractions.

Our recommended hotel to stay in Coimbra is the Hotel: **"Riversuites"**.

Its address is Avenida João das Regras, 80-82, 3040-217 Coimbra, Portugal. Tel.: (00351) 21 824 1055

To Read Reviews of the Hotel on Booking and Book it online, click here. It has a great rating of 8.3 out of 10 in Booking.com and as we have used it many times, we can highly recommend it.

You can expect to pay a price / night of 45€ for a double room. Its modern and contemporary rooms are awesome, the location is spot on nearby the left bank of the Mondego River and the price, as explained above, is appetizing as well, especially for the quality services you're getting.

Hostels:

For those looking for a more budget-friendly option, Coimbra is home to several hostels that offer a range of amenities and services, as well as a fun and social atmosphere. One of the most popular hostels in the city is the Serenata Hostel Coimbra, which is located in the historic center of the city and offers a range of dormitory and private rooms, as well as a communal kitchen and lounge area. Other popular hostels include the HI Coimbra - Pousada de Juventude, which is located near the Mondego River and offers stunning views of the city, and the NS Hostel & Suites, which is located in a historic building and offers a range of private and dormitory rooms.

Guesthouses:

Coimbra is also home to several guesthouses and bed and breakfasts that offer a more personalized and intimate stay, as well as a range of amenities and services. One of the most popular guesthouses in the city is the Casa Morais, which is located near the university and features a range of cozy and comfortable rooms, as well as a communal kitchen and lounge area. Other popular guesthouses include the Casa Pombal, which is set in a historic building and offers a range of rooms and apartments, and the Coimbra Vintage Lofts, which is located in the historic center of the city and features several spacious and stylish lofts.

IV. Aveiro

Located in the heart of Portugal's coastal region, Aveiro is a charming city known for its picturesque canals, colorful boats, and delicious cuisine. Known as the "Venice of Portugal," Aveiro is a popular destination for travelers looking to explore the country's rich history and culture, as well as enjoy some of its most beautiful natural scenery. In this section, we'll explore the top things to see and do in Aveiro, including its top attractions, food and drink, and museums. Whether you're interested in exploring the city's waterways, indulging in some traditional Portuguese dishes, or learning about the region's history and traditions, there's something for everyone in Aveiro.

History and Culture

Aveiro has a rich history and culture that is reflected in its architecture, traditions, and way of life. The city's strategic location on Portugal's coast has made it an important center for trade and commerce throughout history, and it has been influenced by a range of cultures and civilizations over the years.

Aveiro was founded in the 10th century, and it quickly became an important center for fishing and salt production. The city's canals were used to transport salt from the nearby salt flats, and the boats that were used for this purpose are now an iconic symbol of Aveiro's history and culture.

The city was also an important center for trade during the Age of Discovery in the 15th and 16th centuries, and it played a key role in Portugal's global empire. The city's rich history can be seen in its architecture, which features a mix of traditional Portuguese styles and influences from other cultures, including Art Nouveau and Art Deco. Culture in Aveiro:

Aveiro is a city that is proud of its culture and traditions, and there are several festivals and events throughout the year that showcase its unique way of life. One of the most popular festivals is the Festas da

Ria, which takes place in August and celebrates the city's connection to the sea and its fishing traditions.

Another important cultural event is the Carnaval de Aveiro, which takes place in February and features colorful parades and costumes. The city is also known for its traditional crafts, including the famous ovos moles, which are egg-based sweets that are shaped like shells and filled with a sweet egg yolk filling.

Architecture in Aveiro:

Aveiro is a city that is known for its unique architecture, which features a mix of traditional Portuguese styles and influences from other cultures. One of the most iconic examples of this is the Art Nouveau buildings that can be found throughout the city, which feature elaborate facades and intricate details.

Another important example of Aveiro's architecture is the colorful boats that are used to transport salt from the nearby salt flats. These boats, known as moliceiros, are painted in bright colors and feature intricate designs that reflect the city's history and culture.

Museums in Aveiro:

Aveiro is home to several museums that showcase the city's rich history and culture. In this section, we'll explore the top museums in Aveiro, including their top exhibits, website, ticket prices, and address.

1. Museu de Aveiro:

The Museu de Aveiro is located in a former convent and features a range of exhibits that showcase the city's history and culture. The museum has a collection of religious art, including paintings, sculptures, and other artifacts, as well as exhibits on the city's history and traditions.

Top Exhibits:
- The Baroque altarpieces from the convent chapel
- The collection of traditional crafts, including the famous ovos moles

- The archaeological artifacts from the Roman and medieval periods

Website: https://museudeaveiro.cm-aveiro.pt/

Ticket Price: €5 for adults, €3 for students and seniors

Address: Rua João Mendonça, 3810-200 Aveiro, Portugal

2. Museu da Cidade:

The Museu da Cidade is located in the city's former town hall and features exhibits on the history and development of Aveiro. The museum has a range of exhibits, including artifacts from the city's fishing and salt production industries, as well as exhibits on the city's architecture and cultural traditions.

Top Exhibits:

- The collection of moliceiros boats
- The exhibits on the city's Art Nouveau architecture
- The historical artifacts from the city's fishing and salt production industries

Website: http://www.cm-aveiro.pt/pages/460| Ticket Price: Free| Address: Praça da República, 3800-111 Aveiro, Portugal

3. Museu Etnográfico da Região de Aveiro:

The Museu Etnográfico da Região de Aveiro is located in the nearby town of Oliveira do Bairro and is dedicated to preserving and showcasing the region's traditional crafts and way of life. The museum has a range of exhibits, including displays on traditional pottery, lace-making, and farming practices.

Top Exhibits:

- The collection of traditional pottery, including the famous Bordalo Pinheiro ceramics
- The exhibits on lace-making and other traditional crafts
- The displays on farming practices and rural life in the region

Website: https://www.merav.pt/| Ticket Price: €2 for adults, €1 for students and seniors| Address: Rua da Fonte Nova, 3770-204 Oliveira do Bairro, Portugal

Overall, Aveiro is a city with a rich history and culture, and there are several museums in the city and the surrounding region that offer a glimpse into its past and present. Whether you're interested in learning about the city's religious art and architecture, its traditional crafts and industries, or its unique way of life, there's a museum in Aveiro that will suit your interests.

Top Attractions

Aveiro is a city that is full of charm and character, with a range of top attractions that offer visitors a glimpse into its unique history and culture. In this section, we'll explore the top attractions in Aveiro, including its beautiful canals, historic landmarks, and natural scenery.

Ria de Aveiro

One of the most unique and beautiful attractions in Aveiro is the Ria de Aveiro, a lagoon that is connected to the Atlantic Ocean by a narrow channel. The lagoon is home to a range of flora and fauna, including several species of fish, birds, and shellfish.

One of the best ways to explore the Ria de Aveiro is by taking a boat tour, which will allow you to see the lagoon's stunning scenery up close. There are several tour companies in Aveiro that offer boat tours, ranging from short trips around the city's canals to longer excursions that take you out into the open sea.

In addition to boat tours, there are also several hiking and cycling trails that allow you to explore the Ria de Aveiro and its surrounding landscapes. These trails offer stunning views of the lagoon and its wildlife, as well as the opportunity to explore some of the region's historic landmarks and cultural attractions.

One of the most popular hiking trails is the Ecopista do Rio Vouga, which follows the course of the Vouga River and passes through several picturesque towns and villages along the way. The trail is relatively flat and easy to walk or cycle, making it suitable for all fitness levels.

Overall, the Ria de Aveiro is a must-see attraction for anyone visiting Aveiro, offering a unique and beautiful glimpse into the region's natural beauty and wildlife. Whether you're exploring the lagoon by boat, hiking or cycling along its trails, or simply admiring it from a distance, the Ria de Aveiro is sure to leave a lasting impression.

Aveiro canals

One of the most iconic and picturesque attractions in Aveiro is its network of canals, which are often compared to those in Venice, Italy. The canals were originally built in the 19th century to transport goods and people around the city, and they have since become a popular destination for tourists and locals alike.

The canals are lined with colorful houses and buildings, many of which feature traditional Portuguese tiles and Art Nouveau facades. One of the best ways to explore the canals is by taking a traditional moliceiro boat tour, which will take you along the waterways and give you a unique perspective on the city's architecture and history.

The boats are painted in bright colors and often feature intricate designs and patterns, making them a popular subject for photography and a unique symbol of Aveiro's history and culture. The boat tours typically last around 45 minutes to an hour, and they are offered by several tour companies throughout the city.

In addition to boat tours, there are also several walking and cycling paths that allow you to explore the canals and their surroundings. These paths offer stunning views of the waterways and their colorful buildings, as well as the opportunity to explore some of the city's historic landmarks and cultural attractions.

One of the most popular paths is the Rota da Luz, a walking trail that takes you through the historic center of Aveiro and along the canals. The trail is marked by a series of colorful lamps that light up at night, creating a magical and romantic atmosphere.

Overall, the canals of Aveiro are a must-see attraction for anyone visiting the city, offering a unique and beautiful glimpse into its history, culture, and natural scenery. Whether you're exploring the waterways by boat, on foot, or by bike, the canals are sure to leave a lasting impression and make your trip to Aveiro unforgettable.

Costa Nova

Located just a few kilometers from the center of Aveiro, Costa Nova is a charming beachside town that is famous for its colorful houses and beautiful beaches. The town is a popular destination for tourists and locals alike, offering a range of activities and attractions that cater to a variety of interests.

One of the most unique and iconic features of Costa Nova is its row of colorful striped houses, which are known as palheiros. These houses were originally built by fishermen as storage sheds for their fishing gear, but they have since been converted into holiday homes and tourist accommodations.

The palheiros are painted in bright colors and feature intricate stripes and designs, making them a popular subject for photography and a unique symbol of Costa Nova's history and culture. In addition to the palheiros, Costa Nova is also known for its beautiful beaches, which offer miles of golden sand and crystal-clear waters.

One of the most popular beaches in Costa Nova is Praia da Barra, which is located at the mouth of the Aveiro River and offers stunning views of the Atlantic Ocean. The beach is a popular spot for swimming, sunbathing, and water sports, and it also features several bars and restaurants that serve traditional Portuguese dishes and drinks.

In addition to its beaches and palheiros, Costa Nova is also home to several historic landmarks and cultural attractions. One of the most notable is the Farol da Barra, a lighthouse that was built in the 19th century and is now open to visitors. The lighthouse offers stunning views of the surrounding coastline and is a popular spot for sunset watching.

Overall, Costa Nova is a must-see destination for anyone visiting Aveiro, offering a unique and beautiful glimpse into the region's history, culture, and natural beauty. Whether you're exploring the colorful palheiros, relaxing on the golden beaches, or taking in the views from the lighthouse, Costa Nova is sure to leave a lasting impression and make your trip to Aveiro unforgettable.

Food and Drink

Aveiro is a city that is known for its delicious cuisine, which features a range of fresh seafood, traditional Portuguese dishes, and sweet treats. In this section, we'll explore some of the top food and drink options in Aveiro, including its best restaurants, cafes, and bars.

Seafood:

As a coastal city, Aveiro is known for its fresh and delicious seafood, which is a staple of its cuisine. Some of the most popular seafood dishes in Aveiro include grilled sardines, octopus stew, and codfish dishes. One of the best places to try seafood in Aveiro is the Mercado do Peixe, a fish market that is located near the canals and offers a range of fresh fish and seafood that you can buy and prepare yourself.

Restaurants:

Aveiro is home to several top restaurants that offer a range of traditional Portuguese dishes, as well as international cuisine. One of the most popular restaurants in the city is Restaurante O Bairro, which specializes in seafood and offers stunning views of the canals. Other popular restaurants include A Peixaria, which offers traditional Portuguese dishes with a modern twist, and A Tasca do Confrade, which offers a range of regional dishes in a cozy and intimate setting.

Cafes and Bakeries:

Aveiro is also known for its sweet treats, including the famous ovos moles, which are egg-based sweets that are shaped like shells and filled with a sweet egg yolk filling. Some of the best places to try ovos moles in Aveiro include Confeitaria Peixinho, a bakery that has been serving the sweets since 1856, and Fabrica dos Ovos Moles, which offers a range of different flavors and varieties of the traditional sweets.

In addition to ovos moles, Aveiro is also home to several cafes and bakeries that offer a range of other sweet treats and pastries. One of the most popular is A Mulata, a cafe that is known for its delicious cakes and pastries, as well as its cozy and welcoming atmosphere.

Bars:

Aveiro is a city that is known for its vibrant and lively nightlife, with several bars and clubs that offer a range of drinks and entertainment. One of the most popular bars in the city is Bar dos Académicos, which is located near the university and offers a range of drinks and cocktails in a fun and lively atmosphere. Other popular bars include Café Concerto and Antiquus, both of which offer live music and entertainment.

Overall, Aveiro is a city that offers a range of delicious food and drink options, from fresh seafood and traditional Portuguese dishes to sweet treats and lively bars. Whether you're looking to indulge in the local cuisine, relax with a cup of coffee and a pastry, or party the night away, Aveiro has something for everyone.

Nightlife

Aveiro is a city that is known for its lively and vibrant nightlife, with several bars, clubs, and entertainment venues that offer a range of drinks and entertainment. In this section, we'll explore some of the top nightlife spots in Aveiro, including its best bars, clubs, and live music venues.

Bars:

Aveiro is home to several top bars that offer a range of drinks and cocktails, as well as a fun and lively atmosphere. One of the most popular bars in the city is Bar dos Académicos, which is located near the university and offers a range of drinks and cocktails in a fun and lively atmosphere. Other popular bars include Café Concerto, which offers live music and entertainment, and Antiquus, which is known for its extensive drink menu and cozy atmosphere.

Clubs:

For those looking to dance the night away, Aveiro has several clubs that offer a range of music and entertainment. One of the most popular clubs in the city is Mercado Negro, which is located near the canals and offers a range of live music and DJ sets, as well as a lively and energetic atmosphere. Other popular clubs include Bairro Latino, which offers a range of Latin and pop music, and Incógnito, which is known for its electronic music and dance parties.

Live Music:

Aveiro is also home to several live music venues that offer a range of performances, from local and regional bands to international acts. One of the most popular venues in the city is Teatro Aveirense, a historic theater that hosts a range of performances throughout the year, including theater, music, and dance. Other popular live music venues include Café Concerto, which offers live music and entertainment, and Mercado Negro, which hosts regular concerts and performances.

Overall, Aveiro is a city that offers a lively and vibrant nightlife scene, with several bars, clubs, and live music venues that cater to a range of interests and tastes. Whether you're looking to dance the night away, enjoy a few drinks with friends, or take in some live music or entertainment, Aveiro has something for everyone.

Where to Stay in Aveiro

Aveiro is a beautiful coastal city in Portugal that is known for its colorful houses, charming canals, and delicious cuisine. Whether you're visiting Aveiro for a few days or a week, there are plenty of options for accommodation in the city. In this section, we'll explore some of the best places to stay in Aveiro, including hotels, hostels, and guesthouses.

Hotels:

Aveiro is home to several top hotels that offer a range of amenities and services, as well as a comfortable and luxurious stay. One of the most popular hotels in the city is the Hotel Moliceiro, a luxurious 4-star hotel that is located near the canals and features a spa, outdoor pool, and several restaurants. Other popular hotels include the Hotel Imperial, which is located in the heart of the city and offers stunning views of the canals, and the Hotel João Padeiro, which is located near the train station and offers easy access to many of the city's top attractions.

Hostels:

For those looking for a more budget-friendly option, Aveiro is home to several hostels that offer a range of amenities and services, as well as a fun and social atmosphere. One of the most popular hostels in the city is the Aveiro Rossio Hostel, which is located in the historic center of the city and offers a range of dormitory and private rooms, as well as a communal kitchen and lounge area. Other popular hostels include the HI Aveiro - Pousada de Juventude, which is located near the canals and offers stunning views of the city, and the Lemon Tree Hostel, which is located in a historic building and features a range of comfortable and stylish rooms.

Guesthouses:

Aveiro is also home to several guesthouses and bed and breakfasts that offer a more personalized and intimate stay, as well as a range of amenities and services. One of the most popular guesthouses in the city is the **Aveiro City Lodge**, which is located near the canals and features several cozy and comfortable rooms, as well as a communal kitchen and lounge area. Other popular guesthouses include the **Guest House Enaveiro**, which is set in a historic building and features a range of spacious and stylish rooms, and the **Casa do Mercado,** which is located near the fish market and offers a range of rooms and apartments.

V. Day Trips from Coimbra and Aveiro

Coimbra and Aveiro are both beautiful cities in Portugal that offer plenty of attractions, history, and culture. However, if you're looking to explore more of what the region has to offer, there are plenty of great day trip options that are easily accessible from both cities. In this section, we'll explore some of the best day trip options from Coimbra and Aveiro, including historic towns, stunning beaches, and natural parks. Whether you're interested in exploring the region's history and culture or just want to relax and enjoy the beautiful scenery, these day trips are sure to offer a memorable and enjoyable experience.

Figueira da Foz

Located just 40 kilometers from Coimbra, Figueira da Foz is a popular seaside resort town that offers a range of attractions, from stunning beaches to historic landmarks. If you're looking to explore more of the region outside of Coimbra, a day trip to Figueira da Foz is definitely worth considering. In this section, we'll explore why you should visit, a daily itinerary, how to get there, and some things to do and see.

Why visit Figueira da Foz:

Figueira da Foz is a beautiful seaside town that offers a range of attractions and activities for visitors. With its long sandy beaches, historic landmarks, and lively nightlife, Figueira da Foz has something to offer for everyone. Whether you're looking to relax on the beach, explore the town's history and culture, or enjoy some delicious seafood, Figueira da Foz is definitely worth a visit.

Daily itinerary:

08:00 - Start your day with breakfast at one of the local cafes or bakeries, such as Pastelaria Atlântida or Padaria Saudade.

09:00 - Head to the beach and spend the morning soaking up the sun and enjoying the stunning views of the Atlantic Ocean. Some of the most popular beaches in Figueira da Foz include Praia da Claridade, Praia da Figueira, and Praia da Gala.

13:00 - Grab some lunch at one of the local seafood restaurants, such as Restaurante o Caçarola or Restaurante Estrela do Mar.

15:00 - Explore the town's history and culture by visiting some of its historic landmarks, such as the Figueira da Foz Lighthouse or the Santa Catarina Fort.

18:00 - Enjoy some drinks and snacks at one of the town's bars or cafes, such as Cafe Atenas or Bar Oásis.

20:00 - Sample some of the town's delicious seafood at one of its top restaurants, such as Marisqueira Miramar or Restaurante O Casarão.

22:00 - Head back to Coimbra or your accommodation for the night.

How to get there:
Figueira da Foz is easily accessible from Coimbra by both car and train. If you're driving, the journey takes approximately 40 minutes and there are plenty of parking options in the town. If you're taking the train, there are several daily trains that run between Coimbra and Figueira da Foz, with a journey time of approximately 30 minutes.

Things to do and see:
In addition to its beautiful beaches and historic landmarks, Figueira da Foz also offers a range of other attractions and activities for visitors. Some popular things to do and see in the town include visiting the Figueira da Foz Municipal Museum, exploring the town's casino, and taking a boat tour along the Mondego River.

Whether you're interested in history, culture, or just relaxing on the beach, Figueira da Foz has something for everyone.

Bussaco Palace and National Forest

Located just a short distance from both Coimbra and Aveiro, the Bussaco Palace and National Forest offer a stunning combination of natural beauty and historic architecture. If you're looking for a day trip that allows you to explore the great outdoors while also experiencing the region's history and culture, a visit to Bussaco Palace and National Forest is a must. In this section, we'll explore why you should visit, a daily itinerary, how to get there, and some things to do and see.

Why visit Bussaco Palace and National Forest:

The Bussaco Palace and National Forest offer a unique combination of natural beauty and historic architecture, making them a popular destination for visitors to the region. The palace, which was originally built as a royal hunting lodge in the 19th century, is now a luxury hotel that offers stunning views of the forest and surrounding countryside. The forest itself is home to a range of rare and endangered plant and animal species, as well as several walking trails and historic landmarks.

Daily itinerary:

08:00 - Start your day with breakfast at your accommodation in Coimbra or Aveiro.

09:00 - Head to Bussaco Palace and National Forest and spend the morning exploring the forest's walking trails, such as the Mata Nacional do Bussaco Trail or the Vale dos Fetos Trail.

13:00 - Grab some lunch at the Bussaco Palace Hotel, which offers a range of delicious traditional Portuguese cuisine.

15:00 - Explore the palace's historic architecture and stunning gardens, which were designed by renowned landscape architect James William Elmslie.

18:00 - Enjoy some drinks and snacks at the palace's bar or terrace, which offers stunning views of the forest and surrounding countryside.

20:00 - Head back to Coimbra or Aveiro for dinner at one of the local restaurants.

22:00 - End your day by relaxing at your accommodation or exploring the local nightlife.

How to get there:

Bussaco Palace and National Forest are located approximately 35 kilometers from Coimbra and 50 kilometers from Aveiro, and are easily accessible by car or public transportation. If you're driving, the journey takes approximately 45 minutes from Coimbra and 1 hour from Aveiro. If you're taking public transportation, there are several buses that run between Coimbra and Bussaco Palace and National Forest, with a journey time of approximately 1 hour.

Things to do and see:

In addition to exploring the forest's walking trails and the palace's historic architecture and gardens, there are several other things to do and see in Bussaco Palace and National Forest. Some popular attractions include the Palace Chapel, which features stunning stained glass windows and frescoes, and the Cruz Alta viewpoint, which offers panoramic views of the forest and surrounding countryside.

Praia da Barra

Located just a short distance from Aveiro, Praia da Barra is one of the most popular and stunning beaches on the Portuguese coast. With its long stretch of golden sand, clear blue waters, and beautiful lighthouse, Praia da Barra is a must-visit destination for anyone visiting the region. In this section, we'll explore why you should visit, a daily itinerary, how to get there, and some things to do and see.

Why visit Praia da Barra:
Praia da Barra is a beautiful beach that offers a range of activities and amenities for visitors. With its stunning natural beauty, lively atmosphere, and delicious seafood restaurants, Praia da Barra has something to offer for everyone. Whether you're looking to relax on the beach, enjoy some water sports, or explore the town's history and culture, Praia da Barra is definitely worth a visit.

Daily itinerary:
08:00 - Start your day with breakfast at one of the local cafes or bakeries in Aveiro, such as Casa de Chá or Padaria Pãozinho.
09:00 - Head to Praia da Barra and spend the morning soaking up the sun and enjoying the beautiful beach. You can also rent a stand-up paddleboard or surfboard from one of the local rental shops.
13:00 - Grab some lunch at one of the seafood restaurants near the beach, such as Restaurante O Caçarola or Restaurante Praia da Barra.
15:00 - Explore the town's history and culture by visiting the Barra Lighthouse, which is one of the tallest lighthouses in Europe and offers stunning views of the beach and surrounding area.
18:00 - Enjoy some drinks and snacks at one of the beach bars or cafes, such as Casa da Praia or Bar O Pescador.

20:00 - Sample some of the town's delicious seafood at one of its top restaurants, such as Restaurante Cabana do Pescador or Restaurante Barra Velha.

22:00 - Head back to Aveiro or your accommodation for the night.

How to get there:

Praia da Barra is located just 10 kilometers from Aveiro, and is easily accessible by both car and public transportation. If you're driving, the journey takes approximately 15 minutes and there are plenty of parking options near the beach. If you're taking public transportation, there are several buses that run between Aveiro and Praia da Barra, with a journey time of approximately 20 minutes.

Things to do and see:

In addition to enjoying the beach and exploring the Barra Lighthouse, there are several other things to do and see in Praia da Barra. Some popular attractions include the Praia da Costa Nova, which is a nearby beach that features colorful striped houses, and the **Museu Marítimo de Ílhavo**, which offers a range of exhibits on the town's fishing history and culture. Whether you're interested in nature, history, or just enjoying the beach, Praia da Barra has something for everyone.

Ílhavo Maritime Museum

Located just a short distance from Aveiro, the Ílhavo Maritime Museum offers a fascinating insight into the region's fishing history and culture. With its range of exhibits and interactive displays, the museum is a must-visit destination for anyone interested in maritime history or culture. In this section, we'll explore why you should visit, a daily itinerary, how to get there, and some things to do and see.

Why visit Ílhavo Maritime Museum:

The Ílhavo Maritime Museum is one of the most popular and fascinating museums in the region, offering a range of exhibits and interactive displays that explore the region's fishing history and culture. With its range of artifacts, models, and multimedia displays, the museum offers a unique and immersive experience that is both educational and enjoyable.

Daily itinerary:

08:00 - Start your day with breakfast at one of the local cafes or bakeries in Aveiro, such as Casa de Chá or Padaria Pãozinho.

09:00 - Head to the Ílhavo Maritime Museum and spend the morning exploring the museum's exhibits and interactive displays, which cover everything from fishing techniques to the region's maritime history.

13:00 - Grab some lunch at one of the seafood restaurants near the museum, such as Restaurante Casa de Pasto Ponto Final or Restaurante Marisqueira O Caruncho.

15:00 - Explore the nearby town of Ílhavo, which offers a range of historic landmarks and cultural attractions, such as the Igreja da Misericórdia or the Casa da Cultura de Ílhavo.

18:00 - Enjoy some drinks and snacks at one of the local cafes or bars, such as Bar A Barraca or Café Restaurante Avenida.

20:00 - Head back to Aveiro or your accommodation for the night.

How to get there:

The Ílhavo Maritime Museum is located approximately 7 kilometers from Aveiro, and is easily accessible by both car and public transportation. If you're driving, the journey takes approximately 15 minutes and there are plenty of parking options near the museum. If you're taking public transportation, there are several buses that run between Aveiro and Ílhavo, with a journey time of approximately 20 minutes.

Things to do and see:

In addition to exploring the museum's exhibits and interactive displays, there are several other things to do and see in Ílhavo. Some popular attractions include the nearby Costa Nova beach, which features colorful striped houses, and the Museu Vista Alegre, which offers a range of exhibits on the region's ceramics history and culture.

VI. Practical Information

Weather and Best Time to Visit

Coimbra and Aveiro enjoy a Mediterranean climate, with mild temperatures and relatively low rainfall throughout the year. However, the best time to visit depends on your interests and preferences.

The summer months of June to August are the most popular time to visit, as the weather is warm and sunny, and the region's beaches and outdoor activities are at their best. However, this is also the busiest time of year, with larger crowds and higher prices.

Spring and autumn, from March to May and September to November respectively, are also good times to visit, with pleasant temperatures and fewer crowds. This is a great time to explore the region's cities and cultural attractions, and to enjoy outdoor activities such as hiking and cycling.

Winter, from December to February, is the least popular time to visit, as the weather can be cool and rainy, and many of the outdoor attractions are closed. However, this is also the best time to enjoy the region's indoor attractions, such as museums and historic landmarks, and to enjoy the local cuisine and nightlife.

Overall, the best time to visit Coimbra and Aveiro depends on your interests and preferences. If you're looking for a beach vacation or outdoor activities, the summer months are the best time to visit. If you're interested in exploring the region's cities and cultural attractions, spring and autumn are the best times to visit. And if you're looking to enjoy the local cuisine and nightlife, winter is a great time to visit.

How to Get Around

Coimbra and Aveiro are relatively small cities, and many of the top attractions can be easily reached on foot or by bike. However, if you're looking to explore the region more extensively, there are several transportation options available.

Public transportation:

Both Coimbra and Aveiro have efficient and affordable public transportation systems, with buses and trains connecting the cities and surrounding areas. The bus and train schedules and routes can be found on the respective company's websites:

- Coimbra: The local bus company in Coimbra is SMTUC (Serviços Municipalizados de Transportes Urbanos de Coimbra) and the train company is Comboios de Portugal (CP). Bus tickets can be purchased at local bus stations or on board the bus, and train tickets can be purchased at train stations or online. The SMTUC website provides information on routes, schedules, and ticket prices, with prices starting at €1.50 for a single journey. The CP website provides information on train routes, schedules, and ticket prices, with prices starting at €2.55 for a single journey.
- Aveiro: The local bus company in Aveiro is ETAC (Empresa de Transportes António Costa), and the train company is Comboios de Portugal (CP). Bus tickets can be purchased at local bus stations or on board the bus, and train tickets can be purchased at train stations or online. The ETAC website provides information on routes, schedules, and ticket prices, with prices starting at €1.80 for a single journey. The CP website provides information on train routes, schedules, and ticket prices, with prices starting at €2.30 for a single journey.

Tips:

- Consider purchasing a reloadable public transportation card if you plan to use the buses or trains frequently. These cards can be purchased at local stations and can save you money on ticket prices.
- Be sure to check the bus and train schedules in advance, as they may vary depending on the day of the week or time of year.

- When taking the bus, be sure to have the exact change or a reloadable public transportation card, as bus drivers may not have change for larger bills.
- When taking the train, be sure to validate your ticket before boarding the train. Failure to do so can result in a fine.

Taxi:

Taxis are readily available in both Coimbra and Aveiro, and can be easily hailed on the street or booked in advance. In Portugal, taxi fares are regulated by the government, and are generally reasonable. However, it's always a good idea to agree on a price with the driver before starting your journey, especially if you're taking a longer trip.

Prices:

Taxi fares in Coimbra and Aveiro are regulated by the government, and are based on the distance traveled and the time of day. As of 2023, the starting fare for a taxi ride is €3.25 in Coimbra and €3.50 in Aveiro, with an additional charge of €0.47 per kilometer. Taxis also charge extra for night rides, on weekends and holidays, and for luggage.

Booking:

Taxis in Coimbra and Aveiro can be easily hailed on the street, but can also be booked in advance by phone or through a mobile app. Some popular taxi companies in the area include:
- Taxis Coimbra: +351 239 496 496 (Coimbra)
- Taxis Aveiro: +351 234 372 891 (Aveiro)
- Uber: Uber is also available in both Coimbra and Aveiro, and can be booked through the Uber app.

Tips:

- When hailing a taxi on the street, be sure to look for official taxi stands or licensed taxis with a "Táxi" sign on the roof.
- When booking a taxi in advance, be sure to provide the driver with your pickup location and destination, and agree on a fare before starting your journey.

- If you're taking a taxi to or from the airport, be sure to check the estimated fare in advance and agree on a fare with the driver before starting your journey.

Car rental:

If you're looking to explore Coimbra and Aveiro at your own pace, renting a car is a great option. There are several car rental companies located in both cities, including major international chains such as Europcar and Hertz, as well as local companies such as Guerin and AirAuto. Rental prices are generally reasonable, but can vary depending on the time of year and the type of car you choose.

Prices:

Car rental prices in Coimbra and Aveiro vary depending on the car type, rental duration, and time of year. As of 2023, prices for a basic compact car start at around €20 per day, with additional charges for insurance and extras such as GPS and child seats. Rental prices may be higher during peak tourist season or holidays.

Booking:

Car rental companies in Coimbra and Aveiro offer online booking, as well as booking by phone or in person at their offices. Some popular car rental companies in the area include:
- Europcar: https://www.europcar.pt/en/
- Hertz: https://www.hertz.pt/en
- Guerin: https://www.rent-a-car-guerin.com/
- AirAuto: https://www.airauto.pt/en/

Tips:
- Be sure to carefully read the rental agreement and understand the terms and conditions before signing. Some car rental companies may have additional charges or restrictions that you should be aware of.
- Be sure to inspect the car thoroughly before leaving the rental office, and report any damage or issues to the rental company.

- Be aware that parking can be difficult in the city centers, and some of the smaller roads in the surrounding areas may be narrow and winding.
- Be sure to have a valid driver's license and insurance coverage before renting a car in Coimbra or Aveiro.

Bike rental:
Bike rental is a great option for exploring Coimbra and Aveiro, especially if you're looking for a more active and eco-friendly way to get around. Both cities have bike rental companies, and the cities have bike lanes and dedicated cycling paths. However, be aware that some of the region's hills and more rural areas may be challenging for inexperienced cyclists.

Prices:
Bike rental prices in Coimbra and Aveiro vary depending on the type of bike, rental duration, and the company you choose. As of 2023, prices for a basic city bike start at around €10 per day, with discounts for longer rental periods. Some bike rental companies may also offer guided tours and bike accessories such as helmets and locks for an additional fee.

Booking:
Bike rental companies in Coimbra and Aveiro offer online booking, as well as booking by phone or in person at their offices. Some popular bike rental companies in the area include:
- BUGA (Bicicletas Urbanas de Aveiro): http://www.buga.pt/
- Bike a Wish Coimbra: https://www.bikeawish.com/
- GoByBike: https://www.gobybikeportugal.com/

Overall, getting around Coimbra and Aveiro is relatively easy, with several transportation options available. Whether you're looking to explore the cities on foot or bike, or to venture further afield by public transportation or car, there's a transportation option to suit every need and budget.

Safety Tips

Coimbra and Aveiro are generally safe destinations for tourists, with low levels of violent crime. However, as in any city, visitors should be aware of their surroundings and take basic safety precautions to avoid becoming victims of crime or scams.

- Be aware of pickpocketing and theft, especially in crowded tourist areas such as train stations, markets, and popular attractions. Keep your valuables secure and in sight at all times, and be especially cautious of distraction techniques used by pickpockets.
- Avoid walking alone in isolated or unfamiliar areas, especially at night. Stick to well-lit and busy areas, and be aware of your surroundings at all times.
- Use caution when using public transportation, especially at night. If possible, sit in well-lit areas and avoid empty train cars or buses.
- Be cautious of scams, such as people posing as police officers or taxi drivers who overcharge tourists. Always use licensed taxi services and confirm the fare before starting your journey.

Examples of common scams:

- Fake police officers: Scammers may pose as police officers and ask to see your wallet or passport. To avoid falling for this scam, always ask for identification and do not give out personal information or documents.
- Overcharging taxi drivers: Some taxi drivers may overcharge tourists by taking longer routes or charging inflated prices. To avoid this scam, always use licensed taxi services and confirm the fare before starting your journey.
- Distraction techniques: Pickpockets may use distraction techniques, such as bumping into you or asking for directions, to steal your wallet or valuables. To avoid this scam, be aware of your surroundings at all times and keep your valuables secure.

Useful Apps for your Visit

There are several useful apps that can help you make the most of your visit to Coimbra and Aveiro, from finding the best restaurants to navigating public transportation. Here are some of our top picks:

- Google Maps: Google Maps is a must-have app for any traveler, providing detailed maps and directions for walking, driving, and public transportation. The app also includes user reviews and ratings for restaurants, attractions, and hotels.
- TripAdvisor: TripAdvisor is a great app for finding the best restaurants, attractions, and hotels in Coimbra and Aveiro, with user reviews and ratings to help you make informed decisions.
- CP (Comboios de Portugal): The CP app is a great tool for navigating the train system in Portugal, with schedules, ticket prices, and real-time train tracking.
- SMTUC: The SMTUC app is the official app for the bus system in Coimbra, providing schedules, routes, and ticket prices.
- ETAC: The ETAC app is the official app for the bus system in Aveiro, providing schedules, routes, and ticket prices.
- Uber: Uber is available in both Coimbra and Aveiro, providing a convenient and affordable alternative to taxis and public transportation.
- Zomato: Zomato is a great app for finding restaurants in Coimbra and Aveiro, with user reviews, ratings, and menus to help you choose the best dining options.
- Duolingo: If you're not fluent in Portuguese, Duolingo is a great app for learning basic phrases and vocabulary before your trip.

By downloading these apps before your visit, you can easily navigate the cities and make informed decisions about where to eat, what to see, and how to get around.

Useful Phrases

Learning a few basic Portuguese phrases can help you navigate Coimbra and Aveiro with ease, and show locals that you're making an effort to communicate in their language. Here are some useful phrases to get you started:
- Olá: Hello
- Bom dia: Good morning
- Boa tarde: Good afternoon
- Boa noite: Good evening/night
- Obrigado/a: Thank you (male/female)

- Por favor: Please
- Desculpe: Excuse me/sorry
- Com licença: Excuse me/pardon me
- Sim: Yes
- Não: No
- Fala inglês?: Do you speak English?
- Não falo português: I don't speak Portuguese
- Quanto custa?: How much does it cost?
- Onde fica?: Where is it?
- Posso pagar com cartão?: Can I pay with a card?
- Adeus: Goodbye

A 3-Day Itinerary for First Timers

Coimbra and Averio are two beautiful cities located in central Portugal that are rich in history and culture. This three-day itinerary will guide you through the top monuments and attractions that the cities have to offer.

Day 1: Arrival, Top Monuments

10:00 - Arrival at the Coimbra Railway Station or Bus Station.

Since Coimbra has no airport, these are the only gateways to the city. You can arrive in Coimbra Railway Station or in Coimbra Bus Station, depending on your preference regarding these two means of transportation. Both have their own pros and cons. Train is faster but more expensive and, on the other hand, bus is cheaper but way slower. However, the Portuguese bus company Rede Expressos have modern, WiFi equipped and comfortable buses on their fleet, so you'll certainly enjoy a nice ride even if you're travelling on a tight budget.

10:15 - Grab the bus just outside of the station.

The bus is the most convenient way to reach the city center. You can purchase your ticket at the station or directly from the bus driver.

10:35 - Accommodate yourself in the hotel and then visit the city's historic center (Baixa and Alta)

Check in to your hotel and start your day by exploring the historic center of Coimbra. The city's most historic area, Alta & Sofia, which comprises its University and other relevant structures, has a lot to offer to its visitors.

11:00 - Eat a traditional Pastel de Tentúgal in Briosa Cafeteria.

Try the Pastel de Tentúgal, a delicious traditional pastry from Tentúgal. It's a must-try when in Coimbra.

Price: 1€ (approx.)

11:20 - Start climbing the famous Quebra Costas

After passing through the Arch of Almedina, the main entrance or city gate to the protected area of the town, take a walk up the famous Quebra Costas. You'll find many shops, local pastries, and restaurants along the way.

11:45 - Visit the Sé Velha Church and its cloisters

The Sé Velha Church is one of the most important Romanesque monuments in Portugal. Don't forget to visit the cloisters, which are equally impressive.

Ticket Price: 2€ (church + cloisters)

12:30 - Lunch at Tapas Nas Costas

Indulge in one of the best chicken dishes of your life at Tapas Nas Costas. The Portuguese way to cook chicken is called Frango de Churrasco and this is the place to try it.

Address: Tv. de Santo Antão, 11, 1150-312 Lisboa Tel: (00351) 21 342 4389| Price: 8€ - 12€ per person

14:15 - Visit the Museum Machado de Castro

The Museum Machado de Castro is a must-visit for art and history lovers. It's housed in the former Episcopal Palace and showcases a collection of sacred art, ceramics, and sculptures.

Ticket Price: 6€ (Students: 3€)

15:25 - Visit the Sé Nova Church

The Sé Nova Church is one of the most impressive Baroque buildings in Portugal.

Ticket Price: Free

15:45 - Photograph the Porta Férrea and enter the University's Terrace (Pátio das Universidades)

Take a photo of the Porta Férrea, the entrance to the University of Coimbra, and enjoy the views from the terrace.

16:30 - Visit the Joanina Library

The Joanina Library is considered one of the most beautiful libraries in the world and is a must-visit attraction in Coimbra. Located on the campus of the University of Coimbra, this stunning Baroque library was built in the 18th century and is adorned with gold leaf, intricate carvings, and frescoes. Visitors can marvel at the collection of rare books and manuscripts, including the first edition of "Os Lusíadas," Portugal's national epic poem. It's important to note that visitors must purchase a ticket in advance and that photography is not allowed inside the library.

Ticket Price: General Ticket - includes a visit to Hall of Capelos, Private Examination Room, Hall of Arms, Joanina Library, and Academic Prison for only 9€ (Students: 5,50€)

17:30 - Go to the top of "A Cabra"
For a stunning panoramic view of Coimbra, head to the top of "A Cabra," which is the bell tower of the New Cathedral. Climbing the 220 steps to the top is a bit of a workout, but the view is worth it. You'll be able to see the entire city, the Mondego River, and the surrounding hills.
Ticket Price: 1€

18:30 - Stroll down the Monumental Stairs (Escadas Monumentais)
The Monumental Stairs are a grand entrance to the University of Coimbra, with 125 steps leading up to the Paço das Escolas, the main courtyard of the university. Take your time to climb the stairs and admire the ornate sculptures and baroque design.

18:45 - Photograph the Aqueduct of San Sebastian
The Aqueduct of San Sebastian is a magnificent structure that stretches across the city, with 1,570 arches spanning over 18 kilometers. It was built in the 16th century to bring water to the city and is now one of the most iconic landmarks of Coimbra.

19:10 - Spend the rest of the afternoon by walking in the open to public and stress-free Sereia Garden (Jardim da Sereia)

The Sereia Garden is a peaceful oasis in the heart of Coimbra, with fountains, sculptures, and lush greenery. Take a relaxing stroll and enjoy the serenity of the garden.

20:00 - Dinner in one of the various restaurants in Republic Square (Praça da República)
Republic Square is one of the liveliest areas of Coimbra, with a wide variety of restaurants and cafes to choose from. You'll find traditional Portuguese cuisine, as well as international options. Don't miss the opportunity to try Coimbra's famous roasted suckling pig, "leitão assado."
Price: 5€ - 10€ per person

21:30 - Have a drink in one of the various bars located across Republic Square and the descendent street, called Sá da Bandeira Avenue
After dinner, head to one of the bars in the area for a drink or two. Sá da Bandeira Avenue is a popular spot for nightlife, with a variety of bars and clubs to suit every taste.
Price: 1€ - 1,5€ per beer (approx.)

23:00 - Return to your hotel and rest.
After a busy day of sightseeing, it's time to head back to your hotel and rest up for the next day's adventures. The walk back to your hotel should take no more than 10-15 minutes.

1st Day in Coimbra – Map

You can get this map in google maps format online here. Or go to bit.ly/coimbraDay1

ZoomTip 1.1: Transportation

Transportation in Coimbra is mainly done by public bus, operated by SMTUC, or by taxi. However, since your hotel is located close to the city center and its various cultural and historic places, you can easily explore the entire city on foot. Nevertheless, you may need to take the yellow public bus to travel between the Railway Station or the Central Bus Station and the city center. Here's how:

From the Railway Station:

The Railway Station, known as Coimbra B, has a bus stop just outside the station for travelers' convenience.

To reach your hotel, simply take bus 29 and get off at Largo da Portagem or Portagem, near the Santa Clara bridge that crosses the Mondego River. Riversuites Hotel is just a 5-minute walk away by crossing the same bridge and walking around 100 meters. It's a straightforward journey, so don't worry!

From the Central Bus Station:

Also known as Rodoviária de Coimbra, the Central Bus Station has a bus stop just outside the station, similar to the Railway Station.

To reach your hotel, since you're taking the same bus 29, just follow the information specified in the 'Railway Station' section above.

Overall, transportation in Coimbra is relatively easy and convenient, with a reliable bus system and taxi services available. However, walking is a great option for exploring the city center, as it allows you to fully immerse yourself in the city's culture and atmosphere.

ZoomTip 1.2: Information on the Monuments

Sé Velha Church

The Sé Velha Church is an impressive and historic structure that should not be missed by any visitor to Coimbra. Dating back to the 11th century, this church was built just a few years after D. Afonso Henriques declared himself King of Portugal and chose Coimbra as the capital. It is considered one of the most outstanding churches in the city and is a National Monument since 1910.

The architecture of the Sé Velha Church is a blend of Romanesque and Gothic styles, which can be seen in its impressive façade and ornate interior. Visitors can explore the church's three naves and admire its beautiful stained glass windows, intricate carvings, and impressive altar. One of the highlights of a visit to Sé Velha is the cloister, which dates back to the 13th century and is one of the oldest and most beautiful cloisters in Portugal. The cloister's columns and arches are intricately carved and visitors can take a leisurely stroll around the peaceful courtyard.

Admission to the Sé Velha Church and its cloisters is only 2€ and is well worth the price for the stunning architecture and history that can be explored within its walls. Visitors should also take note of the church's opening hours and plan their visit accordingly.

National Museum Machado de Castro

via Sandra Filipe Photography

The National Museum Machado de Castro is a significant art museum in Portugal, named after the renowned Portuguese sculptor, Joaquim Machado de Castro. Located in the University area of Coimbra, the building has functioned as a museum since October 11th, 1913, and underwent extensive renovation from 2006 to 2012. One of the most impressive features of the museum is the Roman Criptoportycus, an ancient underground area that dates back to the 1st century and is located beneath the city of Coimbra.

The museum is open from 10:00 am to 7:00 pm (last entrance 15 minutes before closing) from April to September and from 10:00 am to 1:00 pm / 2:00 pm to 6:00 pm (last entrance 15 minutes before closing) from October to March. It is closed on Mondays, Tuesday mornings, January 1st, Easter Sunday, May 1st, July 4th, and December 25th.
Visitors can expect to pay 6€ for a general ticket, while students can avail of a discounted price of 3€. With its rich history and impressive collection of art and artifacts, the National Museum Machado de Castro is a must-visit attraction in Coimbra.

Sé Nova Church

The *Sé Nova de Coimbra* or, as foreign tourists know it, the New Cathedral of Coimbra, is Coimbra's bishopric seat since 1772, when it was transferred from the Old Cathedral, usually known by many as *Sé Velha*. Dating back from the 17th-century, this amazing Baroque church is located in the heart of the University of Coimbra and is arguably one of the most important religious buildings in whole country. Its interior is delicately decorated with various religious and ancient art pieces, as well with sculptures like the amazing 16th-century Gothic-manueline baptismal font carved by Pero and Felipe Henriques.

Ticket Price: Free

Porta Férrea & School's Courtyard
via Sandra Filipe Photography

Info: The Porta Férrea is a symbolic and ornamented gate that marks the entrance to the main university area and, therefore, to the School's Courtyard since 1634. Built by the famous Portuguese architect António Tavares, the gate depicts some of the most significant members that contributed to the university's foundation, such as D.Dinis and D. João III (both were Kings of Portugal). Passing by the Porta Férrea you'll step in the School's Courtyard, a historic square that represents the heart of the University of Coimbra, which is also a part of the places inscribed in the area classified as a World Heritage Site by UNESCO.

Opening Hours: Always Open - unless there's a significant event going on. | **Ticket Price**: Free

Joanina Library

via Sandra Filipe Photography

The Joanina Library is an extraordinary Baroque library that is located in the School's Courtyard at the heart of the University of Coimbra. This library is a must-visit tourist spot in Coimbra. Built during the reign of João V, King of Portugal, in the 18th century, it houses over 250,000 books and volumes from various fields of study, making it one of the most important libraries in Portugal.

Due to its historical significance, only a maximum of 60 people are allowed inside the Joanina Library at a time. Visitors can also explore the Hall of Capelos, Private Examination Room, Hall of Arms, and Academic Prison as part of the general ticket.

The library is open every day from 8:30 am to 7:00 pm between March 19th to October 31st and from 9:00 am to 5:30 pm between November 1st and March 18th. However, it is closed on January 1st, December

24th, 25th, and 31st. On weekends, it is open from 10:00 am to 4:00 pm.

It is highly recommended to book tickets in advance to avoid the queue. A general ticket costs 9€, while students can avail it at a discounted rate of 5.50€. A visit to the Joanina Library is an unforgettable experience that should not be missed during your trip to Coimbra.

Cabra – University Tower
via Sandra Filipe Photography

The University Clock Tower, commonly referred to as "A Cabra" or the Goat, is an iconic landmark of Coimbra and the highest spot in the city centre. Built between 1728 and 1733, the tower was commissioned by the Italian architect Antonio Canevari and has become one of the most recognizable features of the city.

Don't forget to bring your camera and snap some great photos of the city landscape. Climbing the tower during the evening, especially during the blue hour, is highly recommended and will surely be one of your best experiences in Coimbra.

Opening Hours: March 16th – October 31st: 10:00 am to 6:00 pm
November 1st – March 15th: 10:00 am to 1:00 pm / 2:00 pm to 6:00 pm
Ticket Price: 1€.

Aqueduct of St. Sebastian
via Sandra Filipe Photography

The Aqueduct of St. Sebastian, also known as the Arches of the Garden, is a stunning 16th-century structure located in Coimbra. It replaced the original primitive Roman aqueduct that once stood in the same place. This magnificent piece of architecture is considered a Portuguese National Monument since 1910, and it is a popular spot for tourists and locals alike.

Take some time to admire the impressive arches and the intricate details of the aqueduct. If you have some spare time, enjoy a relaxing afternoon walk in the Botanical Garden, which is located behind the aqueduct. The garden offers a peaceful retreat with a diverse range of flora, and it's an ideal spot for a picnic or to relax after a long day of sightseeing.

Opening Hours: The Aqueduct of St. Sebastian is always open and free to visit.

If you're interested in learning more about the history of the aqueduct, there are guided tours available at specific times of the year. You can check the website of the Coimbra Tourism Office for more information.
Ticket Price: Free

Note: As this is an outdoor attraction, it is recommended to visit during good weather conditions.

ZoomTip 1.3: Tapas Nas Costas

Tapas Nas Costas is a charming restaurant located in the heart of Coimbra on Quebra Costas Street. It's a great spot to try some of the best Portuguese tapas, known as petiscos, which offer a mix of traditional and typical ingredients of Portuguese gastronomy. The restaurant allows you to order a variety of dishes, providing an opportunity to taste a wide range of flavors that will certainly be a highlight of your day.
Price: The average cost per person ranges from 10€ to 15€ depending on how many dishes you order.

Tapas Nas Costas: Rua do Quebra Costas, 19 | 3000-340 Coimbra | Tel: (00351) 239 157 425 | Official Website / Facebook

Day 2: Morning in Coimbra / Arrival in Aveiro

10:00 - Visit the Santa Clara Monastery (Mosteiro de Santa Clara)

View ZoomTip 2.3 | Ticket Price: 5€ (students: 2,5€)

The Santa Clara Monastery, located in the heart of Coimbra, is a historical and religious landmark that dates back to the 14th century. It is home to the tomb of Queen Isabel of Portugal, and features a beautiful Gothic cloister and church.

11:00 - Grab an amazing nutella snack at Nut' Coimbra

After visiting the Santa Clara Monastery, make a pitstop at Nut' Coimbra, a popular café that specializes in delicious Nutella-based treats. Try their signature Nutella crepes or waffles, or indulge in a Nutella hot chocolate.

Price: 2,5€ (approx.)

11:30 - Visit the Santa Cruz Monastery (Mosteiro de Santa Cruz)

View ZoomTip 2.3 | Ticket Price: Free

The Santa Cruz Monastery is one of Coimbra's most iconic landmarks, originally founded in the 12th century. It has undergone numerous renovations over the centuries, but its beautiful Gothic and Baroque architecture remains.

12:30 - Lunch at Dux Taberna Urbana

Head over to Dux Taberna Urbana for a delicious lunch. This trendy restaurant serves up creative Portuguese cuisine, with options like octopus carpaccio, roasted lamb, and homemade burgers. Don't miss out on their signature sangria or gin and tonic cocktails.

Price: Depends on what you choose (Average: 7€ - 10€ per person)

13:30

Return to your hotel, pack your bags and make your way to the Coimbra Railway Station to catch a regional train to Aveiro. The journey takes approximately one hour and is very affordable, making it the perfect option for budget-conscious travelers.

Ticket Price: 5,15€

Attention! Note: If you have a car or are traveling with friends, consider visiting the Aliança Underground Museum before departing Coimbra. View Zoom Tip 2.2 for more information.

15:30

Arrive at Aveiro Railway Station and either walk directly to your hotel (approximately 10 minutes) or take the public bus (Green Line) just outside the station.

15:45

Accommodate yourself in the hotel and visit some of Aveiro's top monuments. Start by checking out the Art Nouveau architecture in the city center, including the famous "Ovos Moles" storefronts.

View ZoomTip 2.1 for more information.

16:15 - Try the famous ovos moles, a traditional pastry from Aveiro Ovos moles, which means "soft eggs" in Portuguese, are a sweet and creamy egg yolk filling wrapped in a thin layer of wafer. It's a traditional pastry from Aveiro, and you can find it in many pastry shops around the city. One of the best places to try this delicacy is at the **Fabrica dos Ovos Moles,** where you can watch the production process and buy some freshly made ovos moles. You can also order them with a cup of expresso for a classic Portuguese combo.
Price: 1,5€ - 2€ (ovo mole + expresso)

16:30 - Visit the Aveiro Museum
The Aveiro Museum, located in the former Convent of Jesus, is a must-visit spot for those interested in the history and culture of Aveiro. The museum's collection includes religious art, archaeological artifacts, and a fascinating exhibit on the history of cod fishing in the region. The convent

itself is also worth exploring, with its beautiful Baroque architecture and lovely cloisters.

View ZoomTip 2.3 | Ticket Price: 4€

18:30 - Stroll through Forum Aveiro

Forum Aveiro is an open-air shopping center located right on one of Aveiro's canals. It's a great place to take a leisurely walk, do some shopping, or simply enjoy the scenery. You can also find several cafes and restaurants here.

19:30 - Dinner in Forum Aveiro

There are several restaurants in Forum Aveiro, serving a variety of cuisines, from traditional Portuguese dishes to international cuisine. One of the best options is the Mercado do Peixe restaurant, which offers fresh seafood dishes with a stunning view of the canal.

Price: 10€ - 20€ per person

22:00 - Return to your hotel and rest

After a busy day of exploring, it's time to rest and recharge for the next day's adventure. If you're feeling adventurous, take a short walk through Aveiro's city center at night to experience the charming city in a different light.

Aliança Underground Museum
via Sandra Filipe Photography

Located in the charming Portuguese village of Sangalhos, situated halfway between Coimbra and Aveiro, the Aliança Underground Museum is a unique and fascinating attraction that every art and wine lover must visit. Spread across approximately 20%-25% of Aliança Vinhos de Portugal's traditional cellars, this museum combines the art of wine-making with extraordinary works of art from renowned sculptors and painters, as well as exhibits of ancient artifacts from various indigenous populations.

The museum was founded in 2007 when the passionate art collector and Portuguese millionaire, Joe Berardo, became the majority shareholder of Aliança Vinhos de Portugal. Berardo saw the cellars as an underexploited space and envisioned the potential for a future museum that would showcase his art collections (also displayed in five other museums!). Since the cellars were subterranean, he decided to give the museum an international and unique touch by designing the entire interior to look like the London Underground network, with a total of eight different "tube stations" (themed exhibitions) during the 1.5-hour, 1.6 km visit.

Opening Hours: Guided tours are available daily at 10:00 am, 11:30 am, 2:30 pm, and 4:00 pm. It is recommended to book your visit in advance since the maximum number of visitors allowed per guided tour is 50. The tours are conducted in Portuguese, English, or French. For reservations, visit their website.

Note: The museum is closed on January 1st, Easter Sunday, and December 25th.

Ticket Price: €3.

Guidora's Top Tip: If you are travelling by car (rented or with friends), the Aliança Underground Museum is a perfect stop to add to your itinerary between Coimbra and Aveiro.

via Sandra Filipe Photography

To book your visit please click here.

Coimbra and Aveiro 2nd Day Map

You can get this map online here. You can also visit bit.ly/CoimbraDay2

ZoomTip 2.3: Information on the Monuments

Monastery of Santa Clara

via Sandra Filipe Photography

The Santa Clara Monastery is a remarkable building that showcases the rich history of Coimbra. Its construction dates back to 1283, and it was rebuilt three years later by the order of Queen Elizabeth, the wife of King Dinis of Portugal, after its dissolution in 1311. Today, the monastery houses a museum and an archaeological site that attract many tourists.

The opening hours for the monastery vary based on the season. From May to September, it is open from 10:00 am to 7:00 pm, and from October to April, it is open from 10:00 am to 5:00 pm. It is closed on Mondays, January 1st, Easter Sunday, May 1st, and December 25th. The ticket price for admission is 5€ for adults and 2.5€ for students.

If you're interested in exploring the history of Coimbra, the Santa Clara Monastery is a must-visit destination.

Monastery of Santa Cruz
via Sandra Filipe Photography

Info: This incredible 12th-century structure is one of the two Portuguese buildings that are granted with the status of National Pantheon, since it houses the tombs of two major and iconic Portuguese Kings: D. Afonso Henriques (the first King of Portugal) and his son D. Sancho I (the second King of Portugal). Constructed between 1132 and 1223, the Monastery of Santa Cruz is arguably one of the most important historical sites not only in the city of Coimbra, but also in the entire country. Given that fact, it was inscribed as a National Monument in the beginning of the 20th-century (1910).

Opening Hours:
Monday-Saturday: 9:00 am to 12:00 pm / 2:00 pm to 5:00 pm Sunday: 4:00 pm to 5:30 pm| *Note:* Civil holidays: Only open during morning.

Ticket Price: Free (To visit the Sacristy, the Chapter House, the Cloisters and temporal expositions – 2,5€ / students: 1,5€)

Museum of Aveiro

via Visit Centro de Portugal Official Website

via Museu de Aveiro Facebook Page

Info: Situated in the old Convent of Jesus of the female Dominican Order, which was commonly known back then as Monastery of Jesus, the Museum of Aveiro houses two different exposition circuits than complement each other: the permanent exhibition and the monumental route. Given the fact that the museum is inserted in a structure dating back from 1465, there are a lot of artifacts and ancient artworks on display, but the Church of Jesus, which is decorated with a luxurious and well-appointed golden woodwork along with some traditional Portuguese ceramics known as *azulejos*, definitely takes center stage.

Opening Hours: Tuesday - Sunday: 10:00 am to 7:00 pm | Closed on Mondays | **Ticket Price**: 4€

Day 3: Cathedral, Moliceiro Cruise and Costa Nova Area

Aveiro, also known as the "Venice of Portugal," is a charming city located along the central coast of Portugal. This day itinerary will take you through some of the city's most iconic landmarks and attractions, providing a glimpse into the history and culture of Aveiro.

10:00 AM: Visit the Aveiro Cathedral, commonly known as Sé de Aveiro or São Domingos Church

The Aveiro Cathedral is a stunning 15th-century Gothic-style church located in the city center. With its intricate architecture and ornate details, the cathedral is a must-see attraction for anyone visiting Aveiro. Admission is free, and visitors are welcome to explore the church's interior and exterior.

11:00 AM: Moliceiro Cruise over the Vouga River Delta

A moliceiro cruise is an excellent way to explore the city's waterways and gain a unique perspective on Aveiro's colorful architecture. These traditional boats were once used to harvest seaweed, but now offer a relaxing and scenic tour of the city's canals. Tickets for a moliceiro cruise cost between €8 and €12.50 per person and can be booked in advance or at the pier.

1:30 PM: Lunch at Mercado do Peixe

Mercado do Peixe is a seafood market located in the city center that also offers a variety of restaurants and eateries. Here you can sample the freshest seafood caught daily by local fishermen. Prices for lunch at Mercado do Peixe range between €18 and €25 per person, depending on the restaurant and menu items.

4:00 PM: Visit the Costa Nova peninsula area

The Costa Nova peninsula is a picturesque area known for its colorful striped houses and stunning beaches. You can easily reach Costa Nova by bus, with a fare of approximately €1.50. Once there, take a leisurely stroll along the beach, or browse the local shops and cafes.

6:00 PM: Snack on another famous pastry of Aveiro known as tripa

Just like ovos moles, tripa is another traditional pastry of Aveiro that you can't miss. Look for the tripa stalls on the Costa Nova boardwalk, where you can find this delicious treat for €1.50 to €2 per piece.

7:00 PM: Dinner at Ramona

Located near two city landmarks, the Aveiro Cathedral and the Museum of Aveiro, Ramona is a burger restaurant that offers around 30 different types of burgers (ranging from €2 to €3.50 each), depending on the ingredients you prefer. This establishment is a fantastic dinner option for your last night in Aveiro. Don't forget to order a large beer, called caneca, to fully experience the Ramona environment.

8:00 PM: Chill in one of the pubs located in Aveiro's historic center

Aveiro's historic center has several street pubs where you can enjoy a drink and soak up the city's vibrant nightlife. They are not far from your hotel, so you can easily walk back when you're ready to call it a night.

11:45 PM: Return to your hotel and rest

After a day of exploring Aveiro, it's time to head back to your hotel and get some rest. Tomorrow you'll need to get up early to head back home, so make sure you get a good night's sleep.

Aveiro 3rd Day Map – Zoomed Out

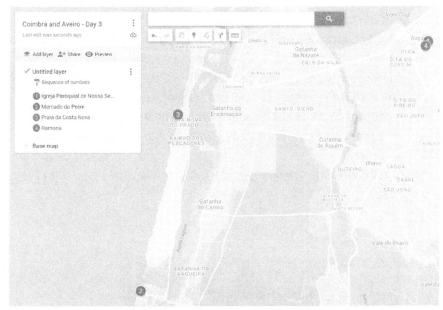

You can get this map online here. You can also visit bit.ly/CoimbraandAveiroDay3

In Day 3 You can also visit: – Barra's Lighthouse, which is the tallest lighthouse in Portugal and of the tallest across the entire European continent, dating back from 1893. Marking the site where the Aveiro Lagoon and its innumerous canals meets the Atlantic Sea, this lighthouse would be easily seen and photographed during on the sections of your third day journey, while visiting the Costa Nova area a few kilometers outside the city center of Aveiro.

Zoom Tip 3.1: Information on the Attractions

Cathedral of Aveiro

Also known as *Igreja de São Domingos* (in English, Church of St. Dominic) or simply *Sé de Aveiro*, the Cathedral of Aveiro is located just a few meters away from the city's museum – Museum of Aveiro. Founded in the early 15th-century (1423) as a Dominican convent, this building is undoubtedly the most important religious structure in the city, which is also registered as a Portuguese National Monument since 1996.

Opening Hours: Monday - Sunday: 9:00 am to 7:00 pm| **Ticket Price**: Free

Moliceiro Cruise
via Onda Colossal Official Website

How to buy tickets: Our recommendation is to buy on one of the company's website (please check them below), in order to get lower prices. There are two major companies doing this traditional cruises (*Onda Colossal* and *Viva a Ria*), so you'll easily find many moliceiro's of those company's while visiting Aveiro.

Info: Every single person that visits Aveiro for its first time has to ride a moliceiro and cruise along the city's narrow canals, just like Amsterdam or Venice. In fact, Aveiro is known as the Portuguese Venice, due to its outstanding similarities with the famous northeastern Italian city. During a the trip, a guide will tell you all the main sites that you'll see on your Vouga River voyage, so you'll get a nice chance to know the city of

Aveiro a little deeper and from a completely different and unique point of view.

Ticket Price: The price varies depending on the cruise you choose – approx. **8€** (duration: *45 minutes*). Please consult both company's websites to check their specific details.

Websites: Onda Colossal & Viva a Ria

Costa Nova

via Travel in Portugal

How to go: Costa Nova is a peninsula located 13km outside Aveiro's city centre. However, it's not difficult to visit the region even without your own means of transportation. Just go to *Rua Clube dos Galitos* (in English, Clube dos Galitos Street) and take the public bus to the beaches, which are also located in the same peninsula. Seasonally, the number of buses could increase, as well as its stops. In conclusion, a "new" bus stop could be closest to your hotel, so we recommend you to ask that information to your hotel receptionist prior to your Costa Nova visit.

Info: Curiously, this tiny peninsula where the Barra Beach and its incredible lighthouse stands on belong to the municipality of Ílhavo, a city in the suburban area of the city of Aveiro. Here you can visit the fish market and various traditional shops and cafes, where the *Tripa de Aveiro* is a must-try pastry for every visitor.

However, the most relevant tourist significance of this area are the traditional houses, known as *palheiros*, which are painted colorful and vibrant vertical or horizontal stripes. Don't forget to take photograph these houses, since they are simply stunning!

Bus Ticket Price: 1,5€ (approx.)

Zoom Tip 3.2: Mercado do Peixe Restaurant

via Sandra Filipe Photography

Info: Located in the first floor of José Estevão's Fish Market, this establishment has its own characteristics that makes it truly unique and absolutely matchless! With a stunning view over one of Aveiro's many canals (in this case, the São Roque canal), this one-of-a-kind restaurant serves the freshest fish and seafood in town, combining it with a refined but cozy atmosphere that will brighten even a cloudy and dark rainy day. It's an unforgettable experience to lunch or dinner in this renowned and award-winner restaurant. **Price:** 18€ - 25€ per person

Honorato: Largo Praça Peixe, 1 |3800-243 Aveiro |Tel: (00351) 234 241 928 |Official Website / Facebook

Food Dishes and Drinks to Try While You are at Coimbra and Aveiro

Below you can find our suggested local Portuguese dishes that you should try in order to enhance your culinary experience, while you are at Porto.

1. Pastel De Nata (in Portuguese): Custard Pie

Pastel de nata, also known as a Portuguese custard tart, is a beloved dessert that has become famous not just in Portugal, but all over the world. This pastry is a delicious treat that is enjoyed by people of all ages and backgrounds.

The history of pastel de nata can be traced back to the early 19th century, when the monks at the Jerónimos Monastery in Lisbon used egg whites to starch their clothes, and the leftover egg yolks were used to make desserts. The monks eventually started selling these desserts to the public, and pastel de nata was born.

Today, you can find pastel de nata in bakeries and cafes all over Portugal. The pastry is made with a crisp, flaky crust that is filled with a sweet, creamy custard made from egg yolks, sugar, milk, and flour. The top of the custard is lightly caramelized, giving it a beautiful golden-brown color.

One of the best places to try pastel de nata is in Lisbon, where the pastry was first created. One popular spot is Pasteis de Belem, a bakery that has been making pastel de nata since 1837. This bakery is known for its delicious custard tarts, which are served warm and sprinkled with cinnamon and powdered sugar.

If you're in other parts of Portugal, don't worry – you can still find delicious pastel de nata. Look for bakeries and cafes that specialize in traditional Portuguese pastries, and be sure to ask for a warm, freshly baked pastry for the best experience.

In addition to being a delicious treat, pastel de nata is also a great way to experience Portuguese culture and history. Whether you're enjoying a pastry in a cozy cafe or taking a bite out of a warm, freshly baked tart on the go, pastel de nata is sure to delight your taste buds and leave you wanting more.

2. Cozido à Portuguesa [Portuguese]: Portuguese Stew

Cozido à Portuguesa, or Portuguese stew, is a traditional dish that is popular all over Portugal. This hearty and flavorful stew is made with a variety of meats and vegetables, making it a perfect comfort food for cold weather or for a hearty meal after a long day of exploring.

The dish is typically made with a variety of meats, including beef, pork, and chicken, as well as smoked sausages like chouriço and morcela. Vegetables like carrots, potatoes, and cabbage are also added, along with white beans and rice.

The stew is typically slow-cooked for several hours, allowing the flavors to meld together and creating a rich and flavorful broth. The meat is typically tender and falling off the bone, while the vegetables are soft and infused with the flavor of the broth.

Cozido à Portuguesa is often served family-style, with a large pot of stew placed in the center of the table and everyone helping themselves. It's a great way to bring people together and enjoy a delicious and hearty meal.

If you're in Portugal, be sure to try Cozido à Portuguesa at a traditional restaurant or tavern. Many restaurants serve the dish on certain days of the week, so be sure to check ahead of time.

3. **Vinho do Porto** [Portuguese]: The famous Port Wine. Try the cellar of Croft.

Vinho do Porto, or Port wine, is a famous fortified wine that originates from the Douro Valley in northern Portugal. This sweet and rich wine has a long and fascinating history, and is still a popular drink both in Portugal and around the world.

Port wine is made from a blend of several different grape varieties, including Touriga Nacional, Tinta Roriz, and Touriga Franca. The grapes are grown in the Douro Valley, which has a unique microclimate that is ideal for producing high-quality wine.

After the grapes are harvested, they are fermented and fortified with brandy, a distilled spirit made from wine. This fortification process stops the fermentation and leaves a sweet, high-alcohol wine with a unique flavor profile.

There are several different styles of Port wine, including Tawny, Ruby, and Vintage. Tawny Port is aged in wooden barrels for several years, giving it a nutty and caramel-like flavor. Ruby Port is aged for a shorter period of time and is characterized by its bright red color and fruity flavor. Vintage Port is made from the best grapes of a single vintage year and is aged for several years in the bottle before it's ready to drink.

Port wine is typically enjoyed as a dessert wine, and is often served with cheese, nuts, or chocolate. It's also a popular ingredient in cocktails, and can be used to add depth and complexity to many different drinks.

4. **Caldo Verde [Portuguese]: Green Broth**

Caldo Verde, or Green Broth, is a traditional Portuguese soup that is beloved throughout the country. This simple and flavorful dish is made with just a few ingredients, but the combination of flavors creates a rich and satisfying soup that's perfect for a cold day.

The main ingredient in Caldo Verde is kale, which is finely chopped and added to a broth made from potatoes, onions, and garlic. The soup is typically finished with a drizzle of olive oil and a few slices of chouriço, a smoked sausage that adds depth and richness to the dish.

Despite its simplicity, Caldo Verde is a deeply satisfying soup that's perfect for a quick lunch or a hearty meal after a day of exploring. It's a popular dish throughout Portugal, and is often served at festivals and other cultural events.

5. Arroz-doce [Portuguese]: Rice Pudding

Arroz-doce, or sweet rice pudding, is a beloved dessert in Portugal and many other countries around the world. This creamy and sweet dish is made with simple ingredients and is often flavored with cinnamon and lemon zest.

The main ingredient in Arroz-doce is short-grain rice, which is cooked in a mixture of milk, sugar, and water until it becomes soft and creamy. The dish is typically flavored with cinnamon sticks and lemon zest, which add a warm and citrusy flavor to the sweet and creamy rice.

Arroz-doce is often served at celebrations and special occasions, and is a staple of Portuguese cuisine. It's a comforting and satisfying dessert that's perfect for a cold day or as a sweet ending to a hearty meal.

In Portugal, Arroz-doce is often served in small cups or bowls, and is sprinkled with cinnamon before serving. It can be served warm or chilled, and is often accompanied by a cup of espresso or a glass of port wine.

If you're in Portugal, be sure to try Arroz-doce at a traditional restaurant or café. It's a classic dessert that's beloved by locals and visitors alike, and is often made with a family recipe that's been passed down for generations.

6. Bacalhau à Zé do Pipo [Pt]: Cod, in Ze do Pipo Style

Bacalhau à Zé do Pipo is a traditional Portuguese dish that features cod fish cooked in a creamy and flavorful sauce. This hearty and delicious dish is beloved throughout Portugal and is often served at family gatherings and special occasions.

The dish is named after a famous Portuguese chef named Zé do Pipo, who is credited with creating the recipe. The dish is made with cod that has been salted and dried, which gives it a distinctive flavor and texture. The cod is then baked in the oven with a layer of mashed potatoes and a creamy sauce made with onions, garlic, cream, and mayonnaise.

The result is a rich and flavorful dish that's creamy and satisfying, with the perfect balance of saltiness and sweetness. Bacalhau à Zé do Pipo is often served with a side of green salad or roasted vegetables, and is best enjoyed with a glass of Portuguese white wine.

7. Queijo Serra da Estrela [Pt]: Serra Da Estrela Cheese

Queijo Serra da Estrela, or Serra Da Estrela Cheese, is a traditional Portuguese cheese that is beloved throughout the country and beyond. This rich and creamy cheese is made from sheep's milk and is often described as one of the best cheeses in the world.

The cheese is named after the Serra da Estrela mountain range in central Portugal, where it has been produced for centuries. The cheese is made from the milk of the Bordaleira sheep, a breed that is native to the region and is known for producing rich and flavorful milk.

Serra Da Estrela Cheese is typically aged for around three months, during which time it develops a creamy and slightly tangy flavor that is unlike any other cheese. The cheese is soft and creamy, with a slightly grainy texture that melts in your mouth.

The cheese is often served as a dessert cheese, either on its own or with a drizzle of honey or a slice of fresh fruit. It's also a popular ingredient in traditional Portuguese dishes, such as the famous Cozido à Portuguesa stew.

8. Ovos Moles de Aveiro [Pt], Soft Eggs from Aveiro [En]

Ovos Moles de Aveiro, which translates to Soft Eggs from Aveiro, is a traditional Portuguese sweet that is especially popular in the city of Aveiro. This delicacy is made from a mixture of egg yolks and sugar, which is then wrapped in a thin layer of rice paper.

The origins of Ovos Moles de Aveiro date back to the 16th century when nuns from local convents began making the sweet as a way to use up the egg yolks left over from starching their habits. Over time, the recipe was perfected and became a beloved local specialty.

Today, Ovos Moles de Aveiro is made by a small number of local producers who use traditional methods to create the delicate and delicious treat. The egg yolks are cooked with sugar over a low heat until they form a thick and creamy custard. This custard is then wrapped in rice paper, which is cut into delicate shapes and decorated with a variety of designs.

Ovos Moles de Aveiro is often served in small wooden barrels, known as barricas, and makes for a delicious dessert or sweet snack. It has a rich and creamy flavor that is balanced by the sweetness of the sugar, and its delicate texture makes it a delight to eat.

If you're visiting Aveiro, be sure to try Ovos Moles de Aveiro at one of the local pastry shops or markets. You can also purchase the sweet as a souvenir to take home with you, as it makes for a unique and delicious gift.

9. **Peixinhos da Horta [Pt], Peixinhos da Horta (Tempura) [En]**

Peixinhos da Horta, which translates to "little fish from the garden," is a traditional Portuguese dish that consists of tempura-battered vegetables. Despite its name, this dish does not actually contain any fish and is entirely vegetarian.

The origins of Peixinhos da Horta can be traced back to the 16th century, when Portuguese traders first encountered tempura during their travels to Asia. The dish was then adapted using local vegetables, and quickly became a popular snack in Portugal.

The most common vegetables used in Peixinhos da Horta include green beans, peppers, and onions, which are coated in a light batter made from flour, water, and eggs. The vegetables are then deep-fried until they are crispy and golden brown.

Peixinhos da Horta is often served as a starter or snack, and is a popular dish during the summer months when vegetables are in abundance. It is typically served with a variety of dipping sauces, such as aioli or sweet chili sauce, and pairs well with a cold beer or glass of white wine.

10. Caldeirada [Pt], Portuguese Fish Stew [En]

Caldeirada, which translates to Portuguese Fish Stew, is a traditional dish that originates from the coastal regions of Portugal. This hearty and flavorful stew is typically made with a variety of fish, potatoes, onions, tomatoes, and herbs.

The dish is believed to have been introduced by Portuguese fishermen who would prepare it on their boats using the catch of the day. The stew was then simmered over an open fire, and the flavors would meld together to create a delicious and satisfying meal.

Today, Caldeirada is still a popular dish in Portugal, and is often served at family gatherings and special occasions. The recipe for Caldeirada varies from region to region, and different types of fish are often used depending on what is available.

Some popular fish used in Caldeirada include cod, hake, and sea bass, and the stew is often flavored with garlic, bay leaves, and paprika. The fish is typically layered with sliced potatoes, onions, and tomatoes, and then simmered in a flavorful broth until the vegetables are tender and the fish is cooked through.

Caldeirada is often served with crusty bread, and pairs well with a crisp white wine or a cold beer. It's a delicious and hearty dish that offers a taste of Portuguese coastal cuisine, and is sure to be a hit with seafood lovers.

Thank you!

We hope you've enjoyed our travel guide to Coimbra and Aveiro. These two cities in Portugal are filled with rich history, stunning architecture, and delicious cuisine. From exploring the impressive university and library in Coimbra to taking a trip to the underground art museum in Aliança Vinhos de Portugal, there's no shortage of activities to do and places to see.

In Aveiro, make sure to take a stroll along the canals and try the famous Ovos Moles pastry. And don't forget to visit the Aveiro Museum and Forum Aveiro for some shopping and dining.

We hope our guide has provided you with all the necessary information to make the most out of your trip. Enjoy your travels and make unforgettable memories in Coimbra and Aveiro!

Copyright Notice

Guidora Coimbra & Aveiro in 3 Days Travel Guide ©

All rights reserved. No part of either publication may be reproduced in any material form, including electronic means, without the prior written permission of the copyright owner.

Text and all materials are protected by UK and international copyright and/or trademark law and may not be reproduced in any form except for non-commercial private viewing or with prior written consent from the publisher, with the exception that permission is hereby granted for the use of this material in the form of brief passages in reviews when the source of the quotations is acknowledged.

Disclaimer

The publishers have checked the information in this travel guide but its accuracy is not warranted or guaranteed. Tokyo visitors are advised that opening times should always be checked before making a journey.

Tracing Copyright Owners

Every effort has been made to trace the copyright holders of referred material. Where these efforts have not been successful, copyright owners are invited to contact the editor (Guidora) so that their copyright can be acknowledged and/or the material removed from the publication.

Creative Commons Content

We are most grateful to publishers of CreativeCommons material, including images. Our policies concerning this material are (1) to credit the copyright owner, and provide a link where possible (2) to remove Creative Commons material, at once, if the copyright owner so requests - for example if the owner changes the licensing of an image.

We will also keep our interpretation of the Creative Commons Non-Commercial license under review. Along with, we believe, most web publishers, our current view is that acceptance of the 'Non-Commercial' condition means (1) we must not sell the image or any publication containing the image (2) we may however use an image as an illustration for some information which is not being sold or offered for sale.

Note to other copyright owners

We are grateful to those copyright owners who have given permission for their material to be used. Some of the material comes from secondary and tertiary sources. In every case we have tried to locate the original author or photographer and make the appropriate acknowledgement. In some cases the sources have proved obscure and we have been unable to track them down. In these cases, we would like to hear from the copyright owners and will be pleased to acknowledge them in future editions or remove the material.

Printed in Great Britain
by Amazon